D0743828

Home

Economics

FOURTEEN ESSAYS BY

Wendell

Berry

NORTH POINT PRESS
FARRAR, STRAUS AND GIROUX
NEW YORK

North Point Press
A division of Farrar, Straus and Giroux
19 Union Square West, New York 10003

Printed in the United States of America
First edition, 1987

LIBRARY OF CONGRESS CATALOG CARD NUMBER: 86–62838
Paperback ISBN: 0-86547-275-0

Designed by David Bullen

www.fsgbooks.com

22   21   20   19   18   17   16   15   14

FOR WES JACKSON

Table of Contents

Preface

I have thought, sometimes, of my essays as trials, not because I think that they render verdicts, but because they make attempts, trying out both their subjects and my understanding. Often, too, they try my patience.

The essays in this book continue an attempt to construct an argument that I began twenty or so years ago. The subject of the argument is the fact, and ultimately the faith, that things connect—that we are wholly dependent on a pattern, an all-inclusive form, that we partly understand. The argument, therefore, is an effort to describe responsibility.

Such an argument is necessarily an *essay*—a trial or an attempt. It risks error all the time; it is in error, inevitably, some of the time. The idea that it could produce a verdict is absurd, as is the possibility that it could be concluded. I am never completely happy with this project, and sometimes I am not happy with it at all. I dislike its necessary incompleteness, and I am embarrassed by its ceaseless insinuation that it is a job for somebody better qualified. I keep returning to it, I think, because the study of connections is an endless fascination, and because the understanding of connections seems to me an indispensable part of humanity's self-defense.

The essays appear here in the order in which they were written, each having been formed under the influence of the ones before. The pattern of the argument, by now, appears to be a sort of irregular spiral; any subject that it has passed through it is likely to pass through again, sometimes saying the same thing in a different way in a different connection, sometimes changing or developing what was said before.

My title is borrowed from a school course, and I do not intend it entirely in fun. Its redundancy seems to acknowledge that what passes now for economics, like what passes now for national defense, has strayed far from any idea of home, either the world or the world's natural ecosystems and human households.

I could not have written essays for so many years without being always more keenly aware both of my own indivisible responsibility for their faults and of the extent to which I must share credit for their virtues. What I write is always an extension of conversations between me and the books I have read and the friends and strangers with whom I have talked. No writer, I think, has been better blessed with friends than I have been. To acknowledge all my debts here would be a daunting task—perhaps an impossible one, since I am sure that I am not aware of all my debts. But I would like to thank at least those friends whose usefulness to this book I know to have been direct: my wife, Tanya (who has been the typist and indispensable critic of every page), my father, my brother, Wes and Dana Jackson, Maurice Telleen, Gene Logsdon, Ed and Cia McClanahan, and Gary Snyder. Angela and John Seymour, Peter Fallon, Loyce Flood, Lancie and Verna Bell Clippinger, and David and Elsie Kline generously provided me with some of my subjects. Nancy Palmer Jones, who copy-edited the manuscript, did me and my readers an immense service. Bill Turnbull, Jack Shoemaker, Tom Christensen, Susanna Tadlock, Kathleen Moses, David Bullen, Lisa Ross, Sharon Ponsford, Jeanne Slater, Rosina Fleming, Bettye

Hemphill, Barbara Stevenson, Emily Heckman, Lisa Levine, Brad Mellema, Kathy McKissock, and other good people at North Point Press have given me helps, comforts, and pleasures that I cannot enumerate, much less repay. I am grateful to them all.

I wish to thank the editors of the following magazines, who published some of these essays in earlier versions, and who have permitted me to reprint them: *Country Journal, Orion Nature Quarterly, Katellagate, Review and Expositor, Whole Earth Review, TriQuarterly, Draft Horse Journal, Land Stewardship Newsletter, Resurgence,* the *L.A. Times Magazine,* and *Wilderness.* "Property, Patriotism and National Defense" was first published as a pamphlet by Hobie and Lois Morris and Guardian Press, and later in *Pushcart Prize, XI,* to the editors of which I am also grateful. "Does Community Have a Value?" was given in London on November 19, 1986, as the seventh Nicholas Bacon Memorial Lecture.

Home

Economics

Letter to Wes Jackson

1982

Port Royal, Kentucky
July 15, 1982

Dear Wes,

I want to try to complete the thought about "randomness" that I was working on when we talked the other day.

The Hans Jenny paragraph that started me off is the last on page twenty-one of *The Soil Resource*:

> Raindrops that pass in random fashion through an imaginary plane above the forest canopy are intercepted by leaves and twigs and channelled into distinctive vert space patterns of through-drip, crown-drip, and stem flow. The soil surface, as receiver, transmits the "rain message" downward, but as the subsoils lack a power source to mold a flow design, the water tends to leave the ecosystem as it entered it, in randomized fashion.

My question is: Does "random" in this (or any) context describe a verifiable condition or a limit of perception?

My answer is: It describes a limit of perception. This is, of course, not a scientist's answer, but it may be that *anybody's* answer would be unscientific. My answer is based on the belief that pattern is verifiable by limited information, whereas the information required to verify randomness is unlimited. As I think you said when we talked, what is perceived as random within a given limit may be seen as part of a pattern within a wider limit.

If this is so, then Dr. Jenny, for accuracy's sake, should have said that rainwater moves from mystery through pattern back into mystery.

If "mystery" is a necessary (that is, honest) term in such a description, then the modern scientific program has not altered the ancient perception of the human condition a jot. If, in using the word "random," scientists only mean "random so far as we can tell," then we are back at about the Book of Job. Some truth meets the eye; some does not. We are up against mystery. To call this mystery "randomness" or "chance" or a "fluke" is to take charge of it on behalf of those who do not respect pattern. To call the unknown "random" is to plant the flag by which to colonize and exploit the known. (A result that our friend Dr. Jenny, of course, did not propose and would not condone.)

To call the unknown by its right name, "mystery," is to suggest that we had better respect the possibility of a larger, unseen pattern that can be damaged or destroyed and, with it, the smaller patterns.

This respecting of mystery obviously has something or other to do with religion, and we moderns have defended ourselves against it by turning it over to religion specialists, who take advantage of our indifference by claiming to know a lot about it.

What impresses me about it, however, is the insistent practicality implicit in it. If we are up against mystery, then we dare act only on the most modest assumptions. The modern scientific program has held that we must act on the basis of knowledge, which, because its effects are so manifestly large, we have assumed to be ample. But if we are up against mystery, then knowledge is relatively small, and the ancient program is the right one: Act on the basis of ignorance. Acting on the basis of ignorance, paradoxically, requires one to know things, remember things—

for instance, that failure is possible, that error is possible, that second chances are desirable (so don't risk everything on the first chance), and so on.

What I think you and I and a few others are working on is a definition of agriculture as up against mystery and ignorance-based. I think we think that this is its *necessary* definition, just as I think we think that several kinds of ruin are the *necessary* result of an agriculture defined as knowledge-based and up against randomness. Such an agriculture conforms exactly to what the ancient program, or programs, understood as evil or hubris. Both the Greeks and the Hebrews told us to watch out for humans who assume that *they* make all the patterns.

Getting Along with Nature

1982

The defenders of nature and wilderness—like their enemies the defenders of the industrial economy—sometimes sound as if the natural and the human were two separate estates, radically different and radically divided. The defenders of nature and wilderness sometimes seem to feel that they must oppose any human encroachment whatsoever, just as the industrialists often apparently feel that they must make the human encroachment absolute or, as they say, "complete the conquest of nature." But there is danger in this opposition, and it can be best dealt with by realizing that these pure and separate categories are pure ideas and do not otherwise exist.

Pure nature, anyhow, is not good for humans to live in, and humans do not want to live in it—or not for very long. Any exposure to the elements that lasts more than a few hours will remind us of the desirability of the basic human amenities: clothing, shelter, cooked food, the company of kinfolk and friends—perhaps even of hot baths and music and books.

It is equally true that a condition that is *purely* human is not good for people to live in, and people do not want to live for very long in it. Obviously, the more artificial a human environment becomes, the more the word "natural" becomes a term of value. It can be argued, indeed, that the conservation movement, as we know it today, is largely a product of the industrial revolution. The people who want clean air, clear streams, and wild forests, prairies, and deserts are the people who no longer have them.

People cannot live apart from nature; that is the first principle of the conservationists. And yet, people cannot live in nature without changing it. But this is true of *all* creatures; they depend upon nature, and they change it. What we call nature is, in a sense, the sum of the changes made by all the various creatures and natural forces in their intricate actions and influences upon each other and upon their places. Because of the woodpeckers, nature is different from what it would be without them. It is different also because of the borers and ants that live in tree trunks, and because of the bacteria that live in the soil under the trees. The making of these differences is the making of the world.

Some of the changes made by wild creatures we would call beneficent: beavers are famous for making ponds that turn into fertile meadows; trees and prairie grasses build soil. But sometimes, too, we would call natural changes destructive. According to early witnesses, for instance, large areas around Kentucky salt licks were severely trampled and eroded by the great herds of hoofed animals that gathered there. The buffalo "streets" through hilly country were so hollowed out by hoof-wear and erosion that they remain visible almost two centuries after the disappearance of the buffalo. And so it can hardly be expected that humans would not change nature. Humans, like all other creatures, must make a difference; otherwise, they cannot live. But unlike other creatures, humans must make a choice as to the kind and scale of the difference they make. If they choose to make too small a difference, they diminish their humanity. If they choose to make too great a difference, they diminish nature, and narrow their subsequent choices; ultimately, they diminish or destroy themselves. Nature, then, is not only our source but also our limit and measure. Or, as the poet Edmund Spenser put it almost four hundred years ago, Nature, who is the "greatest goddesse," acts as a sort of earthly lieutenant of God, and Spenser represents her as both a mother and judge. Her jurisdiction is over the relations between the creatures; she deals "Right to all . . . indifferently," for she is "the equall mother" of all "And knittest each to each, as brother unto brother." Thus, in Spenser, the natural principles of fecundity and order are pointedly linked with the principle of justice, which we may be a little surprised to see that he attributes also to nature. And yet in his insistence on an "indifferent" natural justice, resting on the "brotherhood" of *all* creatures, not just of humans, Spenser would now be said to be on sound ecological footing.

In nature we know that wild creatures sometimes exhaust their vital sources and suffer the natural remedy: drastic population reductions. If lynxes eat too many snowshoe rabbits—which they are said to do repeatedly—then the lynxes starve down to the carrying capacity of their habitat. It is the carrying capacity of the lynx's habitat, not the carrying capacity of the lynx's stomach, that determines the prosperity of lynxes. Similarly, if humans use up too much soil—which they have often done and are doing—then they will starve down to the carrying capacity of *their* habitat. This is nature's "indifferent" justice. As Spenser saw in the sixteenth century, and as we must learn to see now, there is no appeal from this justice. In the hereafter, the Lord may forgive our wrongs against nature, but on earth, so far as we know, He does not overturn her decisions.

One of the differences between humans and lynxes is that humans can see that the principle of balance operates between lynxes and snowshoe rabbits, as between humans and topsoil; another difference, we hope, is that humans have the sense to act on their understanding. We can see, too, that a stable balance is preferable to a balance that tilts back and forth like a seesaw, dumping a surplus of creatures alternately from either end. To say this is to renew the question of whether or not the human relationship with nature is necessarily an adversary relationship, and it is to suggest that the answer is not simple.

But in dealing with this question and in trying to do justice to the presumed complexity of the answer, we are up against an American convention of simple opposition to nature that is deeply established both in our minds and in our ways. We have opposed the primeval forests of the East and the primeval prairies and deserts of the West, we have opposed man-eating beasts and crop-eating insects, sheep-eating coyotes and chicken-eating hawks. In our lawns and gardens and fields, we oppose what we call weeds. And yet more and more of us are beginning to see that this opposition is ultimately destructive even of ourselves, that it does not explain many things that need explaining—in short, that it is untrue.

If our proper relation to nature is not opposition, then what is it? This question becomes complicated and difficult for us because none of us, as I have said, wants to live in a "pure" primeval forest or in a "pure" primeval prairie; we do not want to be eaten by grizzly bears; if we are gardeners, we have a legitimate quarrel with weeds; if, in Kentucky, we are trying to improve our pastures, we are likely to be enemies of the nodding thistle. But, do what we will, we remain under the spell of the primeval forests and prairies that we have cut down and broken; we turn repeatedly and with love to the thought of them and to their surviving remnants. We find ourselves attracted to the grizzly bears, too, and know that they and other great, dangerous animals remain alive in our imaginations as they have been all through human time. Though we cut down the nodding thistles, we acknowledge their beauty and are glad to think that there must be some place where they belong. (They may, in fact, not always be out of place in pastures; if, as seems evident, overgrazing makes an ideal seedbed for these plants, then we must understand them as a part of nature's strategy to protect the ground against abuse by animals.) Even the ugliest garden weeds earn affection from us when we consider how faithfully they perform an indispensable duty in covering the bare ground and in building humus. The weeds, too, are involved in the business of fertility.

We know, then, that the conflict between the human and the natural estates really exists and that it is to some extent necessary. But we are learning, or relearning, something else, too, that frightens us: namely, that this conflict often occurs at the expense of *both* estates. It is not only possible but altogether probable that by diminishing nature we diminish ourselves, and vice versa.

The conflict comes to light most suggestively, perhaps, when advocates for the two sides throw themselves into absolute conflict where no absolute difference can exist. An example of this is the battle between defenders of coyotes and defenders of sheep, in which the coyote-defenders may find it easy to forget that the sheep ranchers are human beings with some authentic complaints against coyotes, and the sheep-defenders find it easy to sound as if they advocate the total eradication of both coyotes and conservationists. Such conflicts—like the old one between hawk-defenders and chicken-defenders—tend to occur between people who use nature indirectly and people who use it directly. It is a dangerous mistake, I think, for either side to pursue such a quarrel on the assumption that victory would be a desirable result.

The fact is that people need both coyotes and sheep, need a world in which both kinds of life are possible. Outside the heat of conflict, conservationists probably know that a sheep is one of the best devices for making coarse foliage humanly edible and that wool is ecologically better than the synthetic fibers, just as most shepherds will be aware that wild nature is of value to them and not lacking in interest and pleasure.

The usefulness of coyotes is, of course, much harder to define than the usefulness of sheep. Coyote fur is not a likely substitute for wool, and, except as a last resort, most people don't want to eat coyotes. The difficulty lies in the difference between what is ours and what is nature's: What is ours is ours because it is directly useful. Coyotes are useful *indirectly,* as part of the health of nature, from which we and our sheep alike must live and take our health. The fact, moreover, may be that sheep and coyotes need each other, at least in the sense that neither would prosper in a place totally unfit for the other.

This sort of conflict, then, does not suggest the possibility of victory so much as it suggests the possibility of a compromise— some kind of peace, even an alliance, between the domestic and the wild. We know that such an alliance is necessary. Most conservationists now take for granted that humans thrive best in ecological health and that the test or sign of this health is the survival of a diversity of wild creatures. We know, too, that we cannot imagine ourselves apart from those necessary survivals of our own wildness that we call our instincts. And we know that we cannot have a healthy agriculture apart from the teeming wilderness in the topsoil, in which worms, bacteria, and other wild creatures are carrying on the fundamental work of decomposition, humus making, water storage, and drainage. "In wildness is the preservation of the world," as Thoreau said, may be a spiritual truth, but it is also a practical fact.

On the other hand, we must not fail to consider the opposite proposition—that, so long at least as humans are in the world, in human culture is the preservation of wildness—which is equally, and more demandingly, true. If wildness is to survive, then *we* must preserve it. We must preserve it by public act, by law, by institutionalizing wildernesses in some places. But such preservation is probably not enough. I have heard Wes Jackson of the Land Institute say, rightly I think, that if we cannot preserve our farmland, we cannot preserve the wilderness. That said, it becomes obvious that if we cannot preserve our cities, we cannot preserve the wilderness. This can be demonstrated practically by saying that the same attitudes that destroy wildness in the topsoil will finally destroy it everywhere; or by saying that if *everyone* has to go to a designated public wilderness for the necessary contact with wildness, then our parks will be no more natural than our cities.

But I am trying to say something more fundamental than that. What I am aiming at—because a lot of evidence seems to point this way—is the probability that nature and human culture, wildness and domesticity, are not opposed but are interdependent. Authentic experience of either will reveal the need of one for the other. In fact, examples from both past and present prove that a human economy and wildness can exist together not only in compatibility but to their mutual benefit.

One of the best examples I have come upon recently is the story of two Sonora Desert oases in Gary Nabhan's book, *The Desert Smells Like Rain*. The first of these oases, A'al Waipia, in Arizona, is dying because the park service, intending to preserve the natural integrity of the place as a bird sanctuary for tourists, removed the Papago Indians who had lived and farmed there. The place was naturally purer after the Indians were gone, but the oasis also began to shrink as the irrigation ditches silted up. As Mr. Nabhan puts it, "an odd thing is happening to their 'natural' bird sanctuary. They are losing the heterogeneity of the habitat, and with it, the birds. The old trees are dying. . . . These riparian trees are essential for the breeding habitat of certain birds. Summer annual seed plants are conspicuously absent. . . . Without the soil disturbance associated with plowing and flood irrigation, these natural foods for birds and rodents no longer germinate."

The other oasis, Ki:towak, in old Mexico, still thrives because a Papago village is still there, still farming. The village's oldest man, Luis Nolia, is the caretaker of the oasis, cleaning the springs and ditches, farming, planting trees: "Luis . . . blesses the oasis," Mr. Nabhan says, "for his work keeps it healthy." An ornithologist who accompanied Mr. Nabhan found twice as many species of birds at the farmed oasis as he found at the bird sanctuary, a fact that Mr. Nabhan's Papago friend, Remedio, explained in this way: "That's because those birds, they come where the people are. When the people live and work in a place, and plant their seeds and water their trees, the birds go live with them. They like those places, there's plenty to eat and that's when we are friends to them."

Another example, from my own experience, is suggestive in a somewhat different way. At the end of July 1981, while I was

using a team of horses to mow a small triangular hillside pasture
that is bordered on two sides by trees, I was suddenly aware of
wings close below me. It was a young red-tailed hawk, who flew up
into a walnut tree. I mowed on to the turn and stopped the team.
The hawk then glided to the ground not twenty feet away. I got off
the mower, stood and watched, even spoke, and the hawk showed
no fear. I could see every feather distinctly, claw and beak and eye,
the creamy down of the breast. Only when I took a step toward
him, separating myself from the team and mower, did he fly. While
I mowed three or four rounds, he stayed near, perched in trees
or standing erect and watchful on the ground. Once, when I
stopped to watch him, he was clearly watching me, stooping to
see under the leaves that screened me from him. Again, when I
could not find him, I stooped, saying to myself, "This is what he
did to look at me," and as I did so I saw him looking at me.

Why had he come? To catch mice? Had he seen me scare one
out of the grass? Or was it curiosity?

A human, of course, cannot speak with authority of the motives of hawks. I am aware of the possibility of explaining the
episode merely by the hawk's youth and inexperience. And yet it
does not happen often or dependably that one is approached so
closely by a hawk of any age. I feel safe in making a couple of
assumptions. The first is that the hawk came because of the con-
junction of the small pasture and its wooded borders, of open
hunting ground and the security of trees. This is the phenomenon
of edge or margin that we know to be one of the powerful attrac-
tions of a diversified landscape, both to wildlife and to humans.
The human eye itself seems drawn to such margins, hungering
for the difference made in the countryside by a hedgy fencerow, a
stream, or a grove of trees. And we know that these margins are
biologically rich, the meeting of two kinds of habitat. But another difference also is important here: the difference between a
large pasture and a small one, or, to use Wes Jackson's terms, the
difference between a field and a patch. The pasture I was mowing
was a patch—small, intimate, nowhere distant from its edges.

My second assumption is that the hawk was emboldened to

come so near because, though he obviously recognized me as a man, I was there with the team of horses, with whom he familiarly and confidently shared the world.

I am saying, in other words, that this little visit between the hawk and me happened because the kind and scale of my farm, my way of farming, and my technology *allowed* it to happen. If I had been driving a tractor in a hundred-acre cornfield, it would not have happened.

In some circles I would certainly be asked if one can or should be serious about such an encounter, if it has any value. And though I cannot produce any hard evidence, I would unhesitatingly answer yes. Such encounters involve another margin—the one between domesticity and wildness—that attracts us irresistibly; they are among the best rewards of outdoor work and among the reasons for loving to farm. When the scale of farming grows so great and obtrusive as to forbid them, the *life* of farming is impoverished.

But perhaps we do find hard evidence of a sort when we consider that *all* of us—the hawk, the horses, and I—were there for our benefit and, to some extent, for our *mutual* benefit: The horses live from the pasture and maintain it with their work, grazing, and manure; the team and I together furnish hunting ground to the hawk; the hawk serves us by controlling the field-mouse population.

These meetings of the human and the natural estates, the domestic and the wild, occur invisibly, of course, in any well-farmed field. The wilderness of a healthy soil, too complex for human comprehension, can yet be husbanded, can benefit from human care, and can deliver incalculable benefits in return. Mutuality of interest and reward is a possibility that can reach to any city backyard, garden, and park, but in any place under human dominance—which is, now, virtually everyplace—it is a possibility that is *both* natural and cultural. If humans want wildness to be possible, then they have to make it possible. If balance is the ruling principle and a stable balance the goal, then, for humans, attaining this goal requires a consciously chosen and deliberately made partnership with nature.

In other words, we can be true to nature only by being true to human nature—to our animal nature as well as to cultural patterns and restraints that keep us from acting like animals. When humans act like animals, they become the most dangerous of animals to themselves and other humans, and this is because of another critical difference between humans and animals: Whereas animals are usually restrained by the limits of physical appetites, humans have mental appetites that can be far more gross and capacious than physical ones. Only humans squander and hoard, murder and pillage because of notions.

The work by which good human and natural possibilities are preserved is complex and difficult, and it probably cannot be accomplished by raw intelligence and information. It requires knowledge, skills, and restraints, some of which must come from our past. In the hurry of technological progress, we have replaced some tools and methods that worked with some that do not work. But we also need culture-borne instructions about who or what humans are and how and on what assumptions they should act. The Chain of Being, for instance—which gave humans a place between animals and angels in the order of Creation—is an old idea that has not been replaced by any adequate new one. It was simply rejected, and the lack of it leaves us without a definition.

Lacking that ancient definition, or any such definition, we do not know at what point to restrain or deny ourselves. We do not know how ambitious to be, what or how much we may safely desire, when or where to stop. I knew a barber once who refused to give a discount to a bald client, explaining that his artistry consisted, not in the cutting off, but in the knowing when to stop. He spoke, I think, as a true artist and a true human. The lack of such knowledge is extremely dangerous in and to an individual. But ignorance of when to stop is a modern epidemic; it is the basis of "industrial progress" and "economic growth." The most obvious practical result of this ignorance is a critical disproportion of scale between the scale of human enterprises and their sources in nature.

The scale of the energy industry, for example, is too big, as is the scale of the transportation industry. The scale of agriculture, from a technological or economic point of view, is too big, but from a demographic point of view, the scale is too small. When there are enough people on the land to use it but not enough to husband it, then the wildness of the soil that we call fertility begins to diminish, and the soil itself begins to flee from us in water and wind.

If the human economy is to be fitted into the natural economy in such a way that both may thrive, the human economy must be built to proper scale. It is possible to talk at great length about the difference between proper and improper scale. It may be enough to say here that that difference is *suggested* by the difference between amplified and unamplified music in the countryside, or the difference between the sound of a motorboat and the sound of oarlocks. A proper human sound, we may say, is one that allows other sounds to be heard. A properly scaled human economy or technology allows a diversity of other creatures to thrive.

"The proper scale," a friend wrote to me, "confers freedom and simplicity . . . and doubtless leads to long life and health." I think that it also confers joy. The renewal of our partnership with nature, the rejoining of our works to their proper places in the natural order, reshaped to their proper scale, implies the reenjoyment both of nature and of human domesticity. Though our task will be difficult, we will greatly mistake its nature if we see it as grim, or if we suppose that it must always be necessary to suffer at work in order to enjoy ourselves in places specializing in "recreation."

Once we grant the possibility of a proper human scale, we see that we have made a radical change of assumptions and values. We realize that we are less interested in technological "breakthroughs" than in technological elegance. Of a new tool or method we will no longer ask: Is it fast? Is it powerful? Is it a labor saver? How many workers will it replace? We will ask instead: Can we (and our children) afford it? Is it fitting to our real needs? Is it becoming to us? Is it unhealthy or ugly? And though we may keep a certain interest in innovation and in what we may become, we will renew our interest in what we have been, realizing that conservationists must necessarily conserve *both* inheritances, the natural and the cultural.

To argue the necessity of wildness to, and in, the human economy is by no means to argue against the necessity of wilderness. The survival of wilderness—of places that we do not change, where we allow the existence even of creatures we perceive as dangerous—is necessary. Our sanity probably requires it. Whether we go to those places or not, we need to know that they exist. And I would argue that we do not need just the great public wildernesses, but millions of small private or semiprivate ones. Every farm should have one; wildernesses can occupy corners of factory grounds and city lots—places where nature is given a free hand, where no human work is done, where people go only as guests. These places function, I think, whether we intend them to or not, as sacred groves—places we respect and leave alone, not because we understand well what goes on there, but because we do not.

We go to wilderness places to be restored, to be instructed in the natural economies of fertility and healing, to admire what we cannot make. Sometimes, as we find to our surprise, we go to be chastened or corrected. And we go in order to return with renewed knowledge by which to judge the health of our human economy and our dwelling places. As we return from our visits to the wilderness, it is sometimes possible to imagine a series of fitting and decent transitions from wild nature to the human community and its supports: from forest to woodlot to the "two-story agriculture" of tree crops and pasture to orchard to meadow to grainfield to garden to household to neighborhood to village to city—so that even when we reached the city we would not be entirely beyond the influence of the nature of that place.

What I have been implying is that I think there is a bad reason to go to the wilderness. We must not go there to escape the ugliness and the dangers of the present human economy. We must not let ourselves feel that to go there is to escape. In the first place, such an escape is now illusory. In the second place, if, even as conservationists, we see the human and the natural economies as necessarily opposite or opposed, we subscribe to the very opposition that threatens to destroy them both. The wild and the domestic now often seem isolated values, estranged from one another. And yet these are not exclusive polarities like good and evil. There can be continuity between them, and there must be.

What we find, if we weight the balance too much in favor of the domestic, is that we involve ourselves in dangers both personal and public. Not the least of these dangers is dependence on distant sources of money and materials. Farmers are in deep trouble now because they have become too dependent on corporations and banks. They have been using methods and species that enforce this dependence. But such a dependence is not safe, either for farmers or for agriculture. It is not safe for urban consumers. Ultimately, as we are beginning to see, it is not safe for banks and corporations—which, though they have evidently not thought so, are dependent upon farmers. Our farms are endangered because—like the interstate highways or modern hospitals or modern universities—they cannot be inexpensively used. To be usable at all they require great expense.

When the human estate becomes so precarious, our only recourse is to move it back toward the estate of nature. We undoubtedly need better plant and animal species than nature provided us. But we are beginning to see that they can be too much better—too dependent on us and on "the economy," too expensive. In farm animals, for instance, we want good commercial quality, but we can see that the ability to produce meat or milk can actually be a threat to the farmer and to the animal if not accompanied by qualities we would call natural: thriftiness, hardiness, physical vigor, resistance to disease and parasites, ability to breed and give birth without assistance, strong mothering instincts. These natural qualities decrease care, work, and worry; they also decrease the costs of production. They save feed and time; they make diseases and cures exceptional rather than routine.

We need crop and forage species of high productive ability also, but we do not need species that will not produce at all without expensive fertilizers and chemicals. Contrary to the premise of agribusiness advertisements and of most expert advice, farmers do not thrive by production or by "skimming" a large "cash flow." They cannot solve their problems merely by increasing production or income. They thrive, like all other creatures, according to the difference between their income and their expenses.

One of the strangest characteristics of the industrial economy is the ability to increase production again and again without ever noticing—or without acknowledging—the *costs* of production. That one Holstein cow should produce 50,000 pounds of milk in a year may appear to be marvelous—a miracle of modern science. But what if her productivity is dependent upon the consumption of a huge amount of grain (about a bushel a day), and therefore upon the availability of cheap petroleum? What if she is too valuable (and too delicate) to be allowed outdoors in the rain? What if the proliferation of her kind will again drastically reduce the number of dairy farms and farmers? Or, to use a more obvious example, can we afford a bushel of grain at a cost of five to twenty bushels of topsoil lost to erosion?

"It is good to have Nature working for you," said Henry Besuden, the dean of American Southdown breeders. "She works for a minimum wage." That is true. She works at times for almost nothing, requiring only that we respect her work and give her a chance, as when she maintains—indeed, improves—the fertility and productivity of a pasture by the natural succession of clover and grass or when she improves a clay soil for us by means of the roots of a grass sod. She works for us by preserving health or wholeness, which for all our ingenuity we cannot make. If we fail to respect her health, she deals out her justice by withdrawing her protection against disease—which we *can* make, and do.

To make this continuity between the natural and the human, we have only two sources of instruction: nature herself and our cultural tradition. If we listen only to the apologists for the industrial economy, who respect neither nature nor culture, we get the idea that it is somehow our goodness that makes us so destructive: The air is unfit to breathe, the water is unfit to drink, the soil is washing away, the cities are violent and the countryside neglected, all because we are intelligent, enterprising, industrious, and generous, concerned only to feed the hungry and to "make a better future for our children." Respect for nature causes us to doubt this, and our cultural tradition confirms and illuminates our doubt: No good thing is destroyed by goodness; good things are destroyed by wickedness. We may identify that insight as Biblical, but it is taken for granted by both the Greek and the Biblical lineages of our culture, from Homer and Moses to William Blake. Since the start of the industrial revolution, there have been voices urging that this inheritance may be safely replaced by intelligence, information, energy, and money. No idea, I believe, could be more dangerous.

Irish Journal

1982

October 6, 1982

For weeks now we have been rushing to prepare for our trip. Then suddenly this afternoon the puzzle of tasks all came together—the new work on the barn and garden was finished, the garden manured and sowed in rye, the winter's wood cut, the suitcases packed—and I had nothing to do. I was here without agenda. It was a kind of homecoming. I walked up through the new pasture and sat under the sycamore above the upper pond. There was noise of traffic on the road, but where I sat it was quiet. The only sound was that of the leaves falling; the only movements were those of the leaves and of the beetles whirling on the surface of the pond.

October 7

Our plane was scheduled to leave Kennedy Airport at 7:20 P.M., and we were on board, ready to leave, at that time—and then sat cramped for two hours in the stench of exhaust fumes, waiting on the runways. When we did finally take off, the crew members proceeded at a pace very considerate of their health through an apparently inflexible routine: instructing the passengers, renting earphones for the movie, selling drinks, and finally serving supper at nearly midnight, home time. Just before I went to sleep I observed a troop of bighorn sheep silently climbing the bulkhead in front of us.

October 8

For me, air travel always has about it an insistent feeling of unreality. I feel that I am where I do not belong, with a totally arbitrary assemblage of other people who do not belong there either. And though I am as much in a hurry as everybody else, I always feel that I am going too fast—*incomprehensibly* fast. It is as though I am being hurried through a time that is destined to remain a simple blank in my life. And the insistence in the voices of captain and crew that this experience is perfectly ordinary only intensifies the suggestion of unreality. To eat one's supper 35,000 feet in the air at a speed of 450 miles per hour is an experience that I have never become prepared for. To sleep at such height and speed is even more improbable. I always wake from such a sleep in the surprise of fearful realization, such as must have been felt in the old days by those who woke knowing that they had been ridden through the sky all night by a witch.

But I did sleep about three hours in spite of the loud talk and laughter of a party of ladies in the seats behind us.

We came down through clouds to sunshine at Shannon Airport at about 8:15. From the air we could see a green, rolling countryside of small pastures divided by hedgerows.

After Kennedy, the Shannon airport seems relaxed and rural. In New York there is a nervous, humorless gearing up to cause great technological events to happen (however late); at Shannon the inclination seems to be to allow them to happen if they must and to accommodate them with as good a humor as possible. People going into the cafeteria for breakfast leave their baggage outside the door, trusting all comers. Although we remain in the ambiance of air travel, we have indeed come a long way from New

York. There is little noise or hurry. The working people make small talk; they know each other and come from the same local life. Officials are friendly to strangers and try to be helpful.

We caught a bus outside the airport and rode the swaying top deck to Limerick, going first past new industrial housing and other signs of "development" and then through some lovely pastureland. At Limerick we took a train for Thurles.

From the train, as it burrowed between hedgerows and embankments, we had glimpses through gates or gaps of little fields, almost all in pasture, until, near Thurles, we began to see wheat and sugar beet fields as well. The beet fields were being harvested; freight cars loaded with beets stood on the sidings, and later we would see huge piles of beets dumped on the roadsides. Most of the cattle we saw were Friesians, the breed we call Holsteins. There were some Herefords and Shorthorns, some that looked like Charolais crosses, a lot of big slaughter steers being finished on pasture. On this part of our trip I saw only one Jersey cow.

We got to Thurles at 1:26 and waited outside the little station for the bus to Cashel, which came at 2:00. The day had turned chilly, damp, and gray, but we were glad to be outdoors. Except for an occasional car or truck or tractor on the road, the town, what we could see of it, was shut and quiet. The only people in sight were a pair of young men a hundred yards away, knocking a ball back and forth in the road with hurling sticks. Peat smoke rose from the chimneys, causing the place to smell stranger to us than it looked.

The station behind us and the little country town in front of us, we were off the main thoroughfares of travel now, the momentum of the flight from New York was playing out, and we could feel the stupor of dislocation. Only a few hours before, we had been at home on our farm on the Kentucky River, and now, having passed through the violences, physical and psychic, of a three-thousand-mile jet flight, we were at Thurles on the River Suir where other people were at home, but we were not. Our age has made a sort of convention of calling these sudden transpositions "wonderful," and, wandering around, so newly come down from the sky onto a distant land, one's thoughts do tend to mutter a little in the jargon of travel ads: "After only a day, here we are at Thurles—isn't it wonderful!" But that is the language of stupe-faction. In actuality, wonder is not what one feels—not as one feels wonder, say, at the flight of a bat or a flock of wild geese. One feels only strange, or so it has been with me. Standing there on the edge of the damp blacktop under the gray sky, I felt present in body but not in mind, my head numb as though stuffed with alien corn. It was as though my mind were still somewhere in the sky over the North Atlantic, hurrying to catch up.

In 1962 when I went from Thurles to Cashel, I had ridden an old wreck of a bus, hauling freight as well as passengers, that had proceeded with a confabulation of squeaks and rattles wild-ly disproportionate to its speed. As it swayed around the curves of the crooked back road, the rear door stood open, admitting the breeze, as though the bus were stationary, a house. In addi-tion to the driver, there was a conductor, a small man who had served principally, it seemed, as greeter of the passengers who boarded at cottages and lane ends all along the way. Between stops he sat with his feet propped up among the bags and boxes, smoking his pipe, a contented householder. This was a local conveyance and did not pretend otherwise. It unloaded country people who had been to Thurles and loaded others who were going to Cashel. When we passed a school, the children leaned over the wall, yelling at us, and the conductor waved.

Twenty years later the bus was a larger, sleeker machine, comic-book modern in design, that brought us to Cashel over the main road, smooth and quiet and fast, no intermediate stops. This was no neighborhood rattletrap that would feel at home wherever it might break down, but a real bus, intent upon getting someplace.

Cashel, too, has changed since I was here twenty years ago. Then one might have called it plain or even drab. It was not the drabness so much of poverty—though there was certainly little of what Americans call affluence—but simply that of an everyday place preoccupied with its everyday life; it was the drabness of work clothes. Now Cashel is bigger. There are many new houses, and many more cars in the streets. The storefronts are now painted in a variety of bright colors. The town has become conscious of how it looks outside to outsiders, has cast off its work clothes, and dressed up. It now obviously thinks of itself as a tourist attraction.

And perhaps it, along with the rest of the Irish Republic, has learned to think of itself as attractive in other ways as well. For in 1973 Ireland joined the European Economic Community and thus initiated an economic boom based on agricultural subsidies, foreign industrial investments, tourist dollars, holiday homes, inflated land prices, and other effects of a flourishing industrial economy. This was Ireland's only period of industrial prosperity, and it lasted only a few years. The boom gave way to recession, as booms are apt to do; in 1980 economic growth almost stopped, real earnings failed to increase, and inflation went to 18 percent. The tourist trade seems also to have declined; before leaving home, we wrote to one of the Cashel hotels for reservations, only to learn that it had already closed for the winter after a disappointing season.

I visited Cashel in 1962 and have come back again because one of my great-grandfathers, James Mathews, came from here. Cashel is the only family source that I know for certain outside of Henry County, Kentucky.

But Cashel is a place of attraction, powerful in aspect and association, beyond anybody's family connections with it. Its great distinction is the Rock of Cashel of Saint Patrick's Rock, which rises three hundred feet out of the Tipperary plain, dominating both the town and miles of lovely countryside and bearing on its crest the ruins of a thirteenth-century cathedral, a tenth-century round tower still perfectly preserved, and, tucked into the angle between the south transept and the choir of the cathedral, Cormac's Chapel, begun in 1127 by Cormac MacCarthaigh, King of Desmond and Bishop of Cashel. And these present buildings, old as they are, belong to a succession of buildings and uses that go back at least to the early fifth century, when Cashel became the seat of the kings of Munster.

At that time, a *caiseal* or stone fort was built on the Rock. There, sometime in the middle of the fifth century, Saint Patrick is said to have baptized King Aengus, thus claiming Munster for Christianity. The story is that during the king's baptism, his foot was inadvertently pierced by the sharp point of the staff that Saint Patrick was leaning on. Afterwards, asked by the saint why he had suffered this in silence, Aengus answered that he had thought it a part of the ritual.

In 1495 the cathedral was burned by the Earl of Kildare, who excused himself to Henry VII on the ground that he had thought the archbishop was inside. Damaged further by Cromwell's men and later restored, the cathedral was finally unroofed and abandoned in the middle of the eighteenth century by one Archbishop Price because it was inaccessible by a coach and four.

The Rock, then, is a place of relics and ruins: fine stonework, carving, and ornamentation that will look strange if one comes to them, as I did the first time, from the churches of Italy and France, but they are at home here both by their own tradition and by the naturalization of weathering and wear.

The best of the buildings on the rock is Cormac's Chapel. Wandering around up there, and again in thought afterwards, one returns to it again and again. There is much about it that is attractive: the high-pitched stone roof, whose steep slopes have a slight outward curve; the contrast between the lightly lifting lines of the roof and the stolid squareness of the transeptal towers; the warmth of the chapel's yellow sandstone against the colder, harder gray of the cathedral walls; the reticence and dignity of its ornamentation; the band of strongly individuated carved heads that follows the rondure of the chancel arch. But what is most attractive, I think, is its scale: It seems exactly as large as it could possibly be without losing something in visual coherence. One experiences the chapel continuously, inside and out, as all of a piece; no part of it can be seen without an awareness of its place in the whole.

Chapel and cathedral and tower are surrounded by graves, some recent, some very old. When I was first here, sheep were grazing among the slabs and crosses. Somewhere among these graves are buried my great-great-grandparents, Edward and Mary Cooney Mathews. All we know of them is their names and their place of burial. Their graves, evidently, were not marked; they were too poor, I suppose, to afford something they needed so little as a gravestone.

On the second day of my visit in 1962, I walked up to the rock in the sunny afternoon to find the place deserted except for the dead, the sheep, and an old man and several boys of the town, who were loafing in the doorway of the cathedral. I sat down with them, for it was a pleasant place, a fine day, and the company was the sort I was used to. And of course I asked the old man if he had ever heard of Edward and Mary Mathews or of their son James who went to America, I guessed, in the 1870s. No, he said, he had not heard of those Mathewses, but he *had* heard of two Mathews brothers who lived back in those days, he thought. One of the brothers was famous as the founder of a temperance society. The other was equally famous as a maker of whiskey; so much whiskey did he make that the cattle that drank at the stream that ran past his place became drunk. The old man had meditated a moment on the symmetry of his tale, which he seemed to find pleasing, for then he had laughed and said, "they canceled each other out," and, after a further moment of meditation, added, "*And* they had the raight."

There was something peculiarly touching to me that day about the presence there of the grazing sheep and the loafers, for then Cashel's past and its present daily life so unassumingly reached to each other for daily reasons. The place's history and its presence were the same.

Now the modern insistence on the past as a presence somehow apart from the present has grown. The sheep are gone, and we could see no traces of them. It was too chilly and drizzly to loaf, but the presence of local idlers in the cathedral door would be more surprising now than it was twenty years ago. The old High Cross of Cashel has been moved indoors to be safe from the weather, its old place now occupied by a replica that attempts to imitate the breakage and weathering of the original. The rock is now obviously perceived as a place for outsiders to visit, not for insiders to stay. And now among the graves are planted flood-lights, so that the old walls, after all their centuries, can be lit up at night.

And yet, though so far dislocated into a past for outsiders, the place still powerfully insists upon its presence in both past and present. Its characteristic voices are still those of crows and jack-daws. The cathedral is still incontestably a ruin not foreseeably to be duplicated by art, possessing a magnanimity and grace unavailable except in ruin. And, however dramatically lighted at night, the old masonry still sprouts tufts of grass and heartsease.

From the roofless central tower of the cathedral, we looked out over a landscape of gently rolling pastureland divided by stone walls and hedgerows, the pastures well shaded, grazing cattle and sheep everywhere. It is a countryside that any lover of grass-land and livestock would feel at home in, and I do look at it with a pleasant sense of familiarity. It is as green, as obviously rich and abounding as the best bluegrass pastures of Kentucky, but is different from them in having been used much longer and far more intimately.

For me, the experience of Cashel comes to rest on a sense of loss, the awareness of being in the presence of a history at once personal and inaccessible. I know that, without knowing when and where, I am crossing paths with my own ancestors, pass-ing the places where they lived and worked, stepping over their graves. I cannot imagine their lives any more than they ever imag-ined the lives of their descendants in Port Royal, Kentucky.

Except for the workers whose scaffolds are set up against the cathedral walls, we were almost the only ones there. We stayed until nearly closing time.

Instead of leaving by the road as we had come, we went down through a pasture where cattle were grazing, and at the foot of the slope, we turned back toward town on a road that took us by the building and pens where the weekly livestock sale is held. From the rock we had seen several blackfaced horned ewes grazing in a small pasture behind the sale barn, and we picked our way through the pens to look at them. They were of the mountain breed that the Irish farmers call "Hornies." I went into the little office in the sale barn and asked about the ewes. The owner or manager told me that they were "mountainy" sheep that belonged to a farmer who had refused the bid he had received on them at last Tuesday's sale and so had left them in hope of doing better next Tuesday. Such sheep, the manager told me, produce a lamb that will dress out at about twenty-five pounds; the Galway, on the other hand, will make a lamb on grass and milk that will reach a carcass weight of fifty pounds.

On our way back to our hotel, we stopped by the harness shop and talked a few minutes with the two harness makers. The workers are repairing the cathedral, they said, because lightning struck it ten or so years ago and made a number of cracks in the walls. It had also knocked loose the huge chunk of masonry now lying below the entrance. I commented on the changes since I was here before. Yes, they said, there have been some prosperous times, but now, with the recession, things are getting back to the way they were. These harness makers live mainly from the racehorse trade, but there were a few workhorse collars lying on the floor to be repaired. Are horses still much used for farmwork? Only in the mountains now, the harness makers said. And the horse carts, which I remembered from my first visit, bringing the milk cans into town in the early mornings at a brisk trot, have now been replaced by trucks that pump the milk from bulk tanks at the farms.

October 9

John Seymour and his wife, Angela, came for us at midmorning, and, after a walk up to the rock with them and coffee at the hotel, we made a leisurely drive to their place near New Ross, going on the back roads by way of Kilkenny. The day was chilly and overcast, but the country we passed through, most of it good farm country, was beautiful.

We stopped to speak over the top of a hedge with a farmer who was loading bagged cider apples into a cart drawn by a large black pony, and later we bought some Spartan apples at a roadside stand. One does not see many orchards anywhere in Ireland, John said, and more are urgently needed. Another urgent need in this country is for more forests.

The general impression is that one is seeing the remains, at least, of a sound, long-term human establishment on the land: The farmsteads are predominantly built of stone, and most of them are old; the fields are almost all divided by hedgerows or stone walls. Most of the country is in pasture, which is sensibly grazed, the stock shifted often from one small field to another. All this is good, and yet farming in Ireland must be looked at in terms of two influences that strongly affect it and that tend to some extent to threaten it: first, the long political and military subjugation of the country by England; and, second, industrialization, which, here as everywhere, has drawn human attention, energy, and affection away from the land.

The best land maintenance, the best livestock husbandry, like the best stone masonry, require excellent local intelligence, locally applied, and applied, for the most part, on a modest scale. Industrial hopes have almost invariably tended to devalue all three: the quality of local intelligence, its local applications, and modesty of scale. A colonial government and its ruling class of alien landlords, on the other hand, may preserve these things, up to a point, insofar as it may find it useful to reward them, but it unavoidably degrades the managerial abilities and virtues in the local people.

Near John's place we stopped to talk with a farmer about his small flock of ewes. They were of a Suffolk-Cheviot cross—Suffolk ram on Cheviot ewe—and there was one Cheviot ewe among them. The farmer said that he clips his pastures once a year and shifts his flock into fresh grass once a week. He was most friendly and gave us several good, small apples, much like the Spartans we had bought earlier.

Blackberries were ripe everywhere in the hedgerows, and the snowberry bushes were showing their small coral blooms.

October 10

Angela and John live at Killowen, a cottage with a small acreage on the valley side above the River Barrow, which at that point divides Wexford from Kilkenny.

We slept in the "caravan" beside the cottage and woke up at 9:00 in sunshine, which did not last long. Angela gave us a big breakfast of ham, eggs, tomatoes, fried bread, and then John drove us to Hook Head, where we spent a good while walking on the rocks below the lighthouse and around the little harbor nearby. Later, we stopped at a pub for crab sandwiches and beer.

Since talking to the man at the sale barn in Cashel, I had been on the lookout for Galway sheep. The farmer we talked to at the end of our trip yesterday told us that there was a flock of Galways nearby, and so, when we left the pub, the sun shining again, we set off to find them.

The sheep turned out to be, not pure Galway, but a Finn-Galway cross. We walked out into the field to look at them, but they would not let us get very close, and then we spent some time talking with the young farmer, his mother, and another woman who was visiting.

The farmer uses a Suffolk ram on the ewes, breeding for January lambs, and is very successful. Last year he lambed over 200 percent. He sells a ninety-pound lamb off grass and milk, with only a small quantity of grain (a "mixed barley meal") fed to the ewes for two or three weeks after lambing. Such flocks of sheep are unusual in this part of the country, where the Suffolk is clearly dominant.

The two women were cutting flowers from the dooryard plots to dry for winter bouquets: strawflowers, bells of Ireland, and hydrangeas. Tanya spoke of the bells of Ireland by name, and the mother looked at her in surprise: "How the hell did *you* know what they are?" They had had trouble learning the name themselves.

The mother, a handsome, young-looking, white-haired lady whose husband is dead, obviously took an active part in the management of the farm. She said that they were giving up grain growing because of the necessity to spray the fields so much. The other woman, a neighbor, had been to America, where, she said, a lot of young people go and do not come back. She said that, during the first part of her three-week visit to Chicago, she had wondered why anyone lived anywhere *but* America. But then she had begun to be bothered by the noise and the crush of people and development and had wanted to get home to Ireland.

The pastures we saw were very good, but the hedgerows were generally disheveled and patched with barbed wire. It is common to see expensive factory-made metal gates tied up with string to the hedgerow bushes.

During the economic boom, with money coming in from Common Market subsidies, some farmers left their old farmstead cottages and built modern "bungalows" out on the paved roads, which undoubtedly added many conveniences to their lives but also added such inconveniences as having to go a long way back lanes or across fields to do the milking and other farm chores.

At work here surely is the country prejudice against country things and the "modern" prejudice against old-fashioned things that one finds everywhere in the United States. These are the prejudices by which the industrial economy is instituted in the minds of individuals—the means by which the individual is divided within and against himself or herself and thus subjugated. Here on the farmland, at the roots of the Irish culture, the industrial economy thus sets up its characteristic division between life and work.

If "convenience" is defined by the industrial economy, it refers first of all to the ease with which one may get to town. If it is defined by an agricultural economy, on the other hand, it refers to the ease with which one may get to one's barn. In dairying, as in any other form of livestock husbandry, that second kind of convenience has practical and economic results. One is less likely to go back to the barn before bedtime to see if a cow is calving if the barn is a mile from the house.

October 11

There was rain during the night and softly falling showers continued off and on through the morning.

After breakfast we walked with John over to a neighbor's milking barn to get a small can of milk from the bulk tank. Our way led along an old lane, once much used but now given up and overgrown; for part of the way it was merely a tunnel through the overhanging wet foliage of the bushes. We walked sometimes in the lane, sometimes in the fields beside it.

The lane goes along the hillside above the Barrow. And as our walk carried us higher, we came to openings from which we could look out across the river at one of the loveliest countrysides that I have ever seen: little hedged fields, mostly in pasture, no two of them the same size or shape, rising from the river's edge over the hills to the horizon. The smallness of the fields contributes greatly to the attractiveness of this country, both visually and agriculturally. This is a small-featured terrain, of many facets or aspects, and it has been understood and divided accordingly, and according also one supposes, to patterns and conveniences of human use. Human use, in imposing certain demands on the land, has accommodated itself to the land's natural shape and character, with the result that the countryside appears both natural and human. It is this balance of the natural and the human that makes a landscape look comfortable and comforting, and this is the work of an old kind of mind, of long attention and familiarity—a mind as different as possible from the industrial or modern mind, which comes into a place, aware only of its own demands, imposing its own geometry. The shapes of these old fields were not laid down by an eye sighting above the surface of the land but by many eyes looking up from and out of an ancient usage and familiarity; they were not imposed on the land but grew out of it.

The neighbor's little milking barn is a part of the stone enclosure of an old farmstead, of which the cottage is now abandoned. The barn is open on the inward side and is small and low-roofed. To be milked, the cows come in two at a time and stand on concrete platforms ten inches or a foot high, the milk being piped from the milkers directly to the bulk tank that is nearby. It is a simple, good, inexpensive setup, but John said it wouldn't pass inspection in England because of its unceiled roof and unplastered stone walls.

On the way back, we took time for a careful look at the hedgerows. These were apparently made by first laying a wall with stones picked up after plowing the adjoining fields; the stones were laid either horizontally or were leaned, rather than laid, together on a slant. Earth was filled in like mortar between and over these stones, and then a thorn hedge was planted along the top.

Though the pastures themselves are generally excellent and well maintained, the hedges and other improvements are deteriorating. A lot of little farmsteads and cottages also are neglected and breaking down. And, of course, the cultural wherewithal is breaking down, too. A potato field we walked through was extremely weedy in spite of the herbicides, which have spared the weeds but, by replacing the work of cultivation, have destroyed the pride and the communal standards that are the only safe or dependable assurance of clean fields.

It is troubling that the farmers should be losing these hedgerows and the little fields that they enclose just as the experts are starting to espouse "strip grazing," a new name for what the farmers have always done here. For, if the deterioration continues, the hedgerows will be lost, since they depend upon an abundance of human energy, interest, and know-how. As the people are lost to the land, the things they have built and kept up on it must be lost, too. One would like to know how many people there are left in the Irish countryside who could build or "lay" a hedge.

The hedgerows will be replaced, one must suppose, by electric fences or by confinement feeding. Either way, the land will be poorer—culturally, aesthetically, and biologically. And economically poorer, too, for the economic importance of the hedgerows is that they exist independent of "the economy." They were not bought, except insofar as they were built for daily wages; but those wages went to the country people, not to a distant city or to "the economy." Electric or wire fencing or the technology of confinement feeding, on the other hand, enriches the city by weakening and impoverishing the country.

Here, in addition to blackberries, there were sloes ripening in the hedgerows. I tasted one; it was quintessentially sour.

In the afternoon John and Angela took us to Kennedy Park, a fine arboretum and the best memorial to John F. Kennedy (whose ancestors lived near here) that I have seen. The park is on the grounds of one of the English estates, the remains of which are very beautiful and include sizable groves of big native trees, a lake with ducks and swans, and a little stream winding between grassy banks, stepping down by a series of artificial waterfalls, each one made to have a look and sound different from the others. One could imagine *The Faerie Queene* performed as a kind of traveling pageant here.

From the park we went to pay a visit to Mrs. Foley, a widow who now shares her cottage with her elderly sister-in-law and her ten-year-old granddaughter. We were welcomed graciously and invited into a room that apparently serves as both dining room and parlor, where Mrs. Foley told us to sit down ("Sit down for yourself," she said to me) while she went off to the kitchen to make tea. While we were waiting, John asked the granddaughter if she would sing for us, and she did sing, with much poise and composure, a very pretty song.

Mrs. Foley soon reappeared and ushered us into the kitchen where she had prepared a pot of tea and set out plates and silverware, bread and butter, two kinds of cookies, and an excellent apple tart. The kitchen was smoky, and she apologized, explaining that a crow had built a nest in the chimney and half stopped it up. John said that he had had the same problem at his place in Wales and had solved it by shooting his shotgun up the chimney, a practice that he strongly recommended to Mrs. Foley.

"Ah, well, but then your chimney was straight," Mrs. Foley said, pronouncing the last word in two syllables: "straigh-et."

Her chimney is indeed crooked—I looked up it—but I liked the fireplace. It is in a sort of alcove, the fire on a flat hearth beneath the chimney opening, a long wooden bench on either side of the hearth. A great iron pot crane is hinged to the wall on the left side of the fire. "That's my hot-water heater," Mrs. Foley said. On either side of the fireplace, the stone masonry has been plastered over and covered with wallpaper bearing a pattern of red brick.

Mrs. Foley is an energetic, entertaining talker, her mind busy among her memories. She loves to speak of farming and farm animals. She said: "I bought a calf for twenty-seven shillings and sixpence. You couldn't buy stockings for that now. She wasn't as big as a pup. I brought her home and she wouldn't eat, so I made a pot of strong tea—with milk and sugar in it, just like for yourself. I put it down her neck, I put it down her neck every hour or two. I put a whole egg, shell and all, down her neck; if there was anything wrong in her stomach, the shell would clean it out. She throve every day. She made the best cow I ever had; she gave more milk, she gave gallons and gallons. I kept her until she couldn't walk; I wouldn't part with her."

John had come to see Mrs. Foley partly to get some cabbage

plants, and in the quickly dimming twilight I walked out with
them into the garden.

This was once a thriving thirty-five-acre farm with grazing
land up on the mountain. In his day, Mr. Foley was a fine gardener
and farmer, and he and Mrs. Foley kept the place both productive
and beautiful. In addition to the farm crops and animals, there
were vegetables and flowers, rose arbors, fruit trees, berry and
currant bushes. The little farmyard and its buildings were kept
up. It was small and abundant, modest and excellent.

Most of the fruit trees have been cut down now, and there are
only small patches of garden; one beautiful flower garden is con-
tained within the walls of a roofless shed. The little stone farmstead is in disarray, the roofs of some of the buildings caving in,
for, now that Mrs. Foley is old, her husband dead, and her son
working in Dublin, there is no one to do the work. There is no
longer any livestock; the mountain pasture is unused.

So now the garden and all are lost, and Mrs. Foley mourns over
it, for she would have it as it was. This is the universal story of
these times. What has vanished at Mrs. Foley's is vanishing in the
rest of Ireland and all over the world. There is no limit to the
sadness of it and no limit, I am afraid, to its cost.

The themes of John's talk about Ireland are its needs for orchards, for kitchen gardens, for truck farms, for forests. In its
hurry to industrialize farming along with everything else, Ireland is losing the ability to produce its own food—and, with
that, its independence. It is importing fruits and vegetables that it
has the soil and climate to produce in abundance for itself.

It is also exporting timber, which, as a country nearly de-
forested, it can ill afford to do. As the cost of fossil fuels has
increased, so, evidently, has the use of wood for fuel but without
any appreciable increase in the planting of trees. It is possible, in
fact, to get a Common Market grant for the *clearing* of forested
land.

From Mrs. Foley's we went to see her daughter, Breda Shannon, and her family. Breda's husband, Dick, is a farmer, who

grows sugar beets, wheat, and barley and does some custom harvesting. He no longer has any livestock. Talking with him was much like talking to an American farmer of the modern type; he had the same complaints about prices and costs.

While we talked of the trials and ills of farming, the children were watching a documentary on Rio de Janeiro on television. Two pairs of very shapely buttocks in bikinis moved slowly across the screen, followed by pictures of starving children.

Back at Killowen, late, Angela gave us soup made of the ink-cap mushrooms that John had spied by the road as we left Kennedy Park.

October 12
We boarded the Dublin bus at Ryan's Pub in New Ross at 9:30 in the morning. It had rained all night, was still raining, and would rain for most of the day. The trip took us through inviting small towns and interesting-looking country, but this is a frustrating way of travel for a farmer, especially with the windows steamed and streaked. One glimpses a thousand things that one would like to stop and look at, only to have them lost in the blur of speed: We saw beautiful pastures with big trees beside a river, a machine harvesting a field of beets in the pouring rain, and a tractor pulling a roller across a pasture.

We were delayed by a traffic jam coming into Dublin, and we did not reach the bus station until about half past one.

We were to meet our friend, the poet and publisher Peter Fallon, at five at the Mont Clare Hotel at Clare Street and Merrion Square, and so we had time on our hands. We crossed the Liffey and ate lunch in a pub near Trinity College; and then we visited the National Library, the National Museum, and the National Gallery, where, as Tanya said, we found the usual plenty of Corots. When we discovered that the Mont Clare Hotel was closed, we waited for Peter in Greene's Bookstore across the street. We were happy to see Peter, his being the first face not new to us in five days—and by then the rain had stopped and the sun was shining.

Peter lives in what was once the head gardener's house on the old estate of Loughcrew near Oldcastle in County Meath, a drive of an hour or so northwest of Dublin. We got there after dark, and, in a country we had never seen and could not see, it was a vivid goodness to enter the lighted, book-filled, friendly rooms of the little house. Peter built fires, brought us drinks and bread and cheese, and left us, at the end of our hurried, noisy day, quiet by the hearth while he prepared us a welcoming supper.

October 13
Morning showed us where we were. Peter's house stands in the highest corner of the old enclosed garden of the Loughcrew estate. It is a small, two-story house of pale yellow brick, its two wings at a right angle conforming to its corner of the garden wall. The wall appears to be twelve or fifteen feet tall, and it encloses four or five acres. There is no longer a garden. The enclosure is grassed, used mainly as a hayfield and sheep pasture, but at this time of year it is used as a pasture for hares by the local coursing club, which rents it for that purpose from Charlie Naper, the owner. The hares are caught in the fields and confined here in preparation for coursing, which will begin later in the fall. At the time we were there, fifteen or so hares were in the garden. By the time coursing would begin, there would be more than a hundred.

The land here is broader featured than that along the River Barrow, and the fields are larger, wide stretches of rolling cropland and green pasture broken by hedgerows, stone fences, and patches of woodland. From the stone wall above the road that runs by Peter's house, the grassed slopes rise with increasing steepness to the tops of the Loughcrew Hills, and you can see cattle and sheep dotted over them.

It was raining again. We had breakfast, sat and talked by the fire in Peter's little stone-floored dining room, and then drove to Oldcastle to shop.

Oldcastle is a nice country town, not conscious of having a great deal to offer to strangers and therefore offering to strangers the pleasantness of any place that is mainly minding its own business and finding it mainly interesting.

Peter's headquarters in Oldcastle is Phil Reilly's Pub. One night at closing time, Peter told us, Phil Reilly was asking his clients to finish their drinks: "Hurry up, please. It's time." Nobody paid attention, and Phil Reilly repeated the call several times, more and more loudly, to no avail. Finally, tired of the noise, Bill Tuite said, "Phil, if you don't stop shouting, we'll go home."

A sign on the wall of Johnny Flood's butcher shop caught my eye: "Great grass makes great beef." This sign is distributed by the Meat Marketing Board, which has mastered the not overly difficult truth that in a grass-growing country the people should eat grass-fed beef. In the United States, also a country with extensive areas superbly suited to grazing, the era of cheap petroleum has produced a long-term glut of cheap corn, ruinous both to farmland and to farmers, and this has in turn produced, according to certified experts, an inflexible preference on the part of "the American housewife" for corn-fed beef. "So much for 'the preference of the American housewife,'" I thought, looking at the sign in the Oldcastle butcher shop, "who so uncannily prefers exactly what the American meat industry prefers that she should prefer."

In the afternoon Peter and Tanya and I walked over to the house of James and Angela Naper. The Loughcrew estate, which in 1880 included twenty thousand acres, has been in the Naper family since the 1640s. Various circumstances have reduced its size, and it has recently been divided among James Naper and his two brothers, James's portion being three hundred acres.

The house and the farmstead where James and his family live speak well of the quality of the work on these old estates. To one used to the comparative flimsiness of farm improvements in most parts of the United States, the improvements on the Naper estate are wonders. The stables are of excellent stonework and carpentry; the stone sheep sheds have foot baths and dipping vats built in; the buildings are set around yards that are enclosed by stone walls and paved with stone. The field gates, which are all about nine feet wide (too narrow by modern standards), are all shop-made of wrought iron and are hinged and latched to heavy stone posts. Everything is made to last indefinitely, which signifies a permanence of intention toward farming and the land such as we have never had at home. This intention may be losing out here, under the various modern pressures, but such marks of it will, one hopes, be slow to vanish. And one hopes that they will be studied and understood, not as relics but as valuable cultural and agricultural achievements, before they are gone. If they can be so understood, they will be preserved and, beyond that, imitated.

We walked out with Angela Naper to look at her horses. She showed us a black gelding that serves the farm as a general-purpose saddle horse, an Irish Draft brood mare, a two-year-old filly, and a pair of two-year-old geldings that will be trained as hunters. The two geldings are kept in a pasture known as the Upper Bull Field. This field lies steeply around the sides of a knoll and, probably for that reason, has never been broken. James told us later that it was once very weedy but was brought back to grass, he thought, by sheep. It is producing abundant pasture now.

On this farm there are three hundred head of crossbred mountain ewes—Cheviot, "Hornies," some Border Leicester—that James is breeding to Suffolk rams. It is hard to get good ewes for breeding, James says, because the ewe lambs sold as breeders tend to be those not good enough for slaughter—a degenerative practice if ever there was one.

The farm also raises cattle and produces crops of wheat and barley. The pastures are invariably excellent and are both harrowed and rolled.

Angela asked us to tea, and while we were at the table I could look out the window at the knoll in the Upper Bull Field where one of the geldings, the reddest one, stood in the last of the sunlight, glowing.

James was building a fence with his hired hand—the two of them had just built a mile of it, of woven wire with a barbed strand at the top—and he did not come in until we had finished tea. We sat in the living room then and talked of farming and other things until about half past eight, when we went back to Peter's house for supper.

James spoke of a time when the estate was fifteen hundred acres and was worked by forty people. Now on his three hundred acres he has only one regular hand. That is a change from thirty-seven and a half acres per hand to one hundred fifty acres per hand.

Fox hunting continues to be a popular sport here, and it is evidently highly productive of antagonisms between hunters and farmers, for a large party on horseback trampling over croplands and jumping with varying success over fences and other obstacles can leave very noticeable damages behind.

Some time ago, the local hunt held a reception at the Naper Arms Hotel in Oldcastle for the local landowners in order to heal any old resentments and to secure forgiveness (or at least tolerance) for any offenses that might be forthcoming. Among the guests was the handyman, Nobby Flanagan, noted for his ability to drink all night and do the hardest of work all day. While Nobby Flanagan was filling himself with brandy and goodwill toward fox hunters, he was approached by the lady who was then "Master of the Hunt":

"Mr. Flanagan, I hope it will be all right for our hunt to cross your land."

"Fire ahead!"

"How *large* is your farm, Mr. Flanagan?"

"Well, if you have a good horse, you can clear it," he said, his "farm" being half an acre in back of his house.

October 14
We drove to Oldcastle early for Peter's mail and then started for Dublin. On our way out of town, we saw Nobby Flanagan himself walking along the side of the road, a very substantial man by his looks.

On our way through the town of Kells, we stopped to see Columcille's House and the round tower, which survive from a monastery built there in the ninth century by monks who were driven from Iona by Norse pirates.

Saint Columcille's or Saint Columba's House is a pleasing, small oratory built of well-laid dark gray stone. It is barrel vaulted and has a steep roof of the same stone as the walls. It measures twenty-three by twenty-one feet by thirty-eight feet tall. That its height so far exceeds its length and breadth makes it an imposing building, even though it is small. A narrow iron stair goes up to a croft between vault and roof. This is divided into three small, low rooms, lit by a window in each gable, where the monks are believed to have slept. If a fire was kept below, then maybe the stones of the vault stayed warm and these rooms were comfortable. If there was no fire, the stones, so high in the wind, must have been bitterly cold.

At Saint Columba's Church (Church of Ireland), we were greeted cordially and shown around by the priest. On the wall was a roster of the priests who had served that church: "550 Columcille . . . 1960 Aidan R. C. Olden."

Among other things of interest on the walls, we found this:

Iona of my heart, Iona of my love, instead of monk's voices shall be the lowing of cattle, but ere the world come to an end Iona shall be as it was.

Near Dublin we drove by a huge field being planted to winter grain. For the last two years, Peter said, it has been planted in barley. It was brown from the roadside to the horizon, cleared of every hedgerow, building, and tree. This is an uncommon sight in Ireland, which helps to make one aware of its fundamental strangeness—the land alienated both from its nature and from its human history. Here, where human habitation on the land has been so long and so comely, there is unusual intensity in one's resentment of such presumption. What had to be removed for this desert to exist?

In Dublin, we went to the Long Room of Trinity College Library to see the Book of Kells. The Long Room itself is worth the trip, and the Book of Kells is surely a supreme work of art. One leans over and ponders it in its glass case with the feeling of having arrived at something both rare and formidable. It cannot, for one thing, be idly or casually looked at. To be seen at all, its intricate artistry must be studied and acknowledged in minute detail; a certain tribute must be paid.

Beautiful and precious as it is, the book must remain in its glass case, rationed to viewers a few pages a day. Though one agrees with the necessity, it is nevertheless frustrating, for the library with its line of tourists is not the proper setting. The proper setting, I suppose, would be a church of the ninth century, like Columcille's House at Kells, where part of the illumination may have been done. But I can only suppose; I can recognize the improper setting, but I cannot guess the proper one. Though the ninth-century building still stands, though some things can be known about it, there seems little chance that we can imagine what it was like when people lived their daily lives in it, thinking of such a book as an intimate and ordinary daily right.

Dublin is greatly changed since I was here in 1962. Over the roofs of the old stone and brick buildings, which gave it, I thought, a unique distinction and character, has risen a new skyline of modern "high rises"—slick, shiny, and characterless. It is as though some Global Village, some Anywheresville, were erupting out of the old city in a monstrous birth. The juxtapositions, overshadowings, and obstructions of prospect are shocking, and they reveal here as elsewhere the fearful contempt for both time and place that characterizes large-scale process.

Peter and I had a literary errand to do, and Tanya wanted to go to the Natural History Museum. We left her there and drove across the city, looking and talking.

Of the House of Columcille and other such buildings, Peter said, "They hadn't time to do poor work." He was talking about the modern inversion of production standards—the prevalent assumption that we haven't time, or can't afford, to work well.

But, of course, nobody ever has time or can ever afford to do poor work; that poor work is affordable is an illusion created by the industrial economy. If bad work is done, a high price must be paid for it; all "the economy" can do is forward the bill to a later generation—and, in the process, make it payable in suffering.

Peter showed me the new campus of University College, Dublin, which, as he said, could as readily be "a community college in Minnesota," just as the barley field we saw in the morning would look equally at home in Iowa and as the new Dublin high rises would stand as credibly in any city in any "developed" country in the world.

On the other hand, Cormac's Chapel and Columcille's House and the little fields along the Barrow all belong where they are.

The modern faith in individual genius is advertised in those high rises and in that agricultural desert. This is not the contradiction it seems to be, for individual genius of the modern kind never has courage equal to its essential loneliness, and so it commits itself passionately to clichés of individualism and a uniformity of innovation, ignorant of what precedes it, destructive of what it ignores.

But the real genius of a country, though it may indeed fructify in great individual geniuses, is in the fine abilities—in the minds, eyes, and hands—of tens of thousands of ordinary workers. Peter called this "the genius of genus." Columcille's House was not, like a monument of modern architecture, the work only of one individual genius but grew out of many miles of stone walls around little fields and out of many cottages.

Thus, coming to Ireland has reminded me again how long, complex, and deep must be the origins of the best work of any kind.

Among other natural wonders at the museum, Tanya heard a guard, off in a corner, singing "Some Enchanted Evening" in a very pretty tenor, and she saw a stuffed specimen of our redbird (*Richmondena cardinalis*) identified as a "Virginia nightingale."

The sun shone all day.

October 15

In bright morning sunlight we went to the hilltop opposite James Naper's house to visit the Loughcrew Cairns, driving part of the way in Peter's car and then walking. On the steep upper slopes of the hill, the turf is spongy, a wispy moss growing among the grass. We saw several hares as we walked along, and below us lay the remains of an ancient circular fort.

Along two ridges of the Loughcrew Hills are thirty cairns of the type known as "passage graves." They have been there for about forty-five hundred years. The burial chamber consists of a central aisle or passage with offsets defined by standing slabs. This interior structure was then mounded over with small stones and turf, and the mound was encircled by a curb of slabs set on end. In one of the smaller cairns, now roofless, the interior is cross-shaped, having only two offsets. In another, which we entered through the eastward-facing doorway, there are several offsets, but it is nevertheless a small enclosure with no room wasted on grandeur. Some of the slabs bear concentric circular patterns shallowly incised. These are signs, surely, but their significance is lost. Here is a past that, except for these dumb stones and signs and a few other artifacts now removed, has almost entirely gone out of reach. It is easy to think that some of Peter's ancestors helped with this work—even that some of mine did. But who were they, what did they look like, how did they live, what did they believe? All of them and all their time have entered the world of the dead to which these graves made a passage. The imagination reaches for a hold of some kind but finds none; it is like looking through glass.

And how significant it seemed to turn from that darkness and step out through the stone doorway onto the surface of the earth again, the sunlit country lying all around.

Tanya and Peter went back to the car and left me to walk down from the cairns through the pastures to meet them on the road in front of James and Angela's house.

It was a lovely morning, and the quiet—the absence of human voices, a rare occurrence on this trip—seemed nearly palpable. I made a leisurely descent of it, coming down across excellent pastures where sheep and cattle were grazing, past the stone fences and other enduring works of the old Loughcrew estate and the wire fences of our own time. The green slope was dotted in places with the brown foliage of gorse bushes that had been cut down and left lying. I thought of the possibility, for native inhabitants of an old country, of a preserved and preserving continuity from an unknown past—ancient burial mounds growing grass, grazed by sheep—through a remembered past to the present. I came out onto the road by one of the wrought-iron gates where a fine big ash stands by the stone wall.

When Peter and Tanya picked me up, we drove to the town of Trim, where a weekly livestock sale is held, and spent a long time watching the auction and wandering among the sheep pens. The sheep were nearly all crossbred, though we did see a few Cheviots, four Texel rams, and (at last) a pen of Galways, which are good-looking large sheep with a topknot of wool. There were also a great many pens of the little mountain sheep, "Hornies," that come from the West. These are coarse-wooled horned ewes, of mixed colors, black and gray and white, that appeared to weigh about sixty pounds. The prices for them were not good; when they were auctioned, there was some rejecting of bids, followed by a great deal of dickering.

James Naper, who had come with a load of lambs, joined us, and he and Peter introduced us to several of the farmers, all of whom were friendly and eager to have us pleased with Ireland and the day and the sale. One of them, hearing that we raise Cheviots at home and were interested in seeing sheep of that breed, said: "Now here is a pen of *pure* Cheviots. Well, not *wholly* pure, but they're Cheviots."

The place for Cheviots in Ireland is said to be County Wicklow, and we did see a good many of them there as we came up from New Ross to Dublin on the bus.

In the evening, in Phil Reilly's Pub, we met Tom Tilson, a grave-faced bespectacled man in workman's clothes, who is the hero of a story that Peter told us on the way home.

One Christmas day Tom Tilson and some others were drinking in a bar that was officially closed, as the law requires all bars to be on that day. Everybody had got well filled by the spirit of the occasion when Tom said he had to go home; his sister would have dinner ready. Having studied him closely, his companions decided that he could not make the trip alone, and one of them went along to see that he was delivered to his sister, safe and sound. No sooner had this kind friend returned to the bar than there was a knock. Expecting the police, the company hastily set the place to rights, concealed the evidence, and cautiously opened the door. It was Tom Tilson.

"I just want to buy a drink," he said, "for the man who left me home."

Higher Education
and Home Defense

1983

Several years ago, I attended a meeting in Madison, Indiana, that I have been unable to forget, it seems so emblematic of the fate of our country in our time. In the audience at that meeting were many citizens of local communities, my own among them, who were distrustful of the nuclear power plant then being built (but now discontinued) at Marble Hill. Seated on the stage were representatives of Public Service Indiana, the company that was building the power plant, and members of the Nuclear Regulatory Commission, whose job it presumably was to protect us from the acknowledged dangers of the use of nuclear power, as well as from the already recognized deceits and ineptitudes of Public Service Indiana.

The meeting proceeded as such meetings typically proceed. The fears, objections, questions, and complaints of the local people were met with technical jargon and with bland assurances that the chance of catastrophe was small. In such a confrontation, the official assumption apparently is that those who speak most incomprehensibly and dispassionately are right and that those who speak plainly and with feeling are wrong. Local allegiances,

personal loyalties, and private fears are not scientifically respect-
able; they do not weigh at all against "objective consideration of
the facts"—even though some of the "facts" may be highly speculative or even false. Indeed, in the history of such confronta-
tions, the victories have mainly gone to the objective considerers
of the so-called facts.

Those considerers were then still winning at Marble Hill, even
though the fraud and incompetence of Public Service Indiana
was a matter of public record. But that meeting produced one
question and one answer that tell us all we need to know about
the nature of such an enterprise, and about the role of education
in it. A lady rose in the audience and asked the fifteen or twenty
personages on the stage to tell us how many of them lived within
the fifty-mile danger zone around Marble Hill. The question
proved tactically brilliant, apparently shocking the personages
on the stage, who were forced to give it the shortest, plainest
answer of the evening: *Not one.* Not a single one of those well-
paid, well-educated, successful, important men would need to
worry about his family or his property in the event of a catastrophic mistake at Marble Hill.

This story would be less interesting if it were unusual. My
point, of course, is that it is *not* unusual. Some version of it is now
happening in this country virtually everywhere, virtually every
day. Everywhere, every day, local life is being discomforted, dis-
rupted, endangered, or destroyed by powerful people who live,
or who are privileged to think that they live, beyond the bad
effects of their bad work.

A powerful class of itinerant professional vandals is now pil-
laging the country and laying it waste. Their vandalism is not
called by that name because of its enormous profitability (to
some) and the grandeur of its scale. If one wrecks a private home,
that is vandalism, but if, to build a nuclear power plant, one
destroys good farmland, disrupts a local community, and jeopar-
dizes lives, homes, and properties within an area of several thousand square miles, *that* is industrial progress.

The members of this prestigious class of rampaging professionals must meet two requirements. The first is that they must be the purest sort of careerists—"upwardly mobile" transients who will permit no stay or place to interrupt their personal advance. They must have no local allegiances; they must not have a local point of view. In order to be able to desecrate, endanger, or destroy a *place*, after all, one must be able to leave it and to forget it. One must never think of any place as one's home; one must never think of any place as anyone else's home. One must believe that no place is as valuable as what it might be changed into or as what might be taken out of it. Unlike a life at home, which makes ever more particular and precious the places and creatures of this world, the careerist's life generalizes the world, reducing its abundant and comely diversity to "raw material."

I do not mean to say that people with local allegiances and local points of view can have no legitimate interest in energy. I do mean to say that their interest is different in both quality and kind from the present *professional* interest. Local people would not willingly use energy that destroyed its natural or human source or that endangered the user or the place of use. They would not believe that they could improve their neighborhoods by making them unhealthy or dangerous. They would not believe that it could be necessary to destroy their community in order to save it.

The second requirement for entrance into the class of professional vandals is "higher education." One's eligibility must be certified by a college, for, whatever the real condition or quality of the minds in it, this class is both intellectual and elitist. It proposes to do its vandalism by thinking; insofar as its purposes will require dirty hands, *other* hands will be employed.

Many of these professionals have been educated, at considerable public expense, in colleges or universities that had originally a clear mandate to serve localities or regions—to receive the daughters and sons of their regions, educate them, and send them home again to serve and strengthen their communities. The outcome shows, I think, that they have generally betrayed this mandate, having worked instead to uproot the best brains and talents, to direct them away from home into exploitative careers in one or another of the professions, and so to make them predators of communities and homelands, their own as well as other people's.

Education in the true sense, of course, is an enablement to *serve*—both the living human community in its natural household or neighborhood and the precious cultural possessions that the living community inherits or should inherit. To educate is, literally, to "bring up," to bring young people to a responsible maturity, to help them to be good caretakers of what they have been given, to help them to be charitable toward fellow creatures. Such an education is obviously pleasant and useful to have; that a sizable number of humans should have it is probably also one of the necessities of human life in this world. And if this education is to be used well, it is obvious that it must be used some *where;* it must be used where one lives, where one intends to continue to live; it must be brought home.

When educational institutions educate people to *leave* home, then they have redefined education as "career preparation." In doing so, they have made it a commodity—something to be *bought* in order to make money. The great wrong in this is that it obscures the fact that education—real education—is free. I am necessarily well aware that schools and books have a cost that must be paid, but I am sure nevertheless that what is taught and learned is free. None of us would be so foolish as to suppose that the worth of a good book is the same as the money value of its paper and ink or that the worth of good teaching could be computed in salaries. What is taught and learned is free—priceless, but free. To make a commodity of it is to work its ruin, for, when we put a price on it, we both reduce its value and blind the recipient to the obligations that always accompany good gifts: namely, to use them well and to hand them on unimpaired. To make a commodity of education, then, is inevitably to make a kind of weapon of it because, when it is dissociated from the sense of obligation, it can be put directly at the service of greed.

The people on the stage at the Marble Hill meeting may have thought of themselves as "public servants." But they were servants, at best, of the *general* public, which means, in practice, that they might be enemies at any time to any particular segment of the general public. As servants of the "general good," they stood ready to sacrifice the good of any particular community or place—which, of course, is a way of saying that they had no reliable way to distinguish between the public interest and their own. When they appeared before us, they were serving their own professional commitment and their own ambition. They had not come to reassure us so far as they honestly could do so or to redress our just grievances. They had not come even to determine if our grievances were just. They had come to mislead us, to bewilder us with the jargon of their expertise, to imply that our fears were ignorant and selfish. Their manner of paying attention to us was simply a way of ignoring us.

That meeting, then, was not really a meeting at all but one of the enactments of a division that is rapidly deepening in our country: a division between people who are trying to defend the health, the integrity, even the existence of places whose values they sum up in the words "home" and "community," and people for whom those words signify no value at all.

Two Economies

I

Some time ago, in a conversation with Wes Jackson in which we were laboring to define the causes of the modern ruination of farmland, we finally got around to the money economy. I said that an economy based on energy would be more benign because it would be more comprehensive.

Wes would not agree. "An energy economy still wouldn't be comprehensive enough."

"Well," I said, "then what kind of economy *would* be comprehensive enough?"

He hesitated a moment, and then, grinning, said, "The Kingdom of God."

I assume that Wes used the term because he found it, at that point in our conversation, indispensable; I assume so because, in my pondering over its occurrence at that point, I have found it indispensable myself. For the thing that troubles us about the industrial economy is exactly that it is not comprehensive enough, that, moreover, it tends to destroy what it does not comprehend, and that it is *dependent* upon much that it does not comprehend. In attempting to criticize such an economy, we naturally pose against it an economy that does not leave anything out, and we can say without presuming too much that the first principle of the Kingdom of God is that it includes everything; in it, the fall of every sparrow is a significant event. We are in it whether we know it or not and whether we wish to be or not. Another principle, both ecological and traditional, is that everything in the Kingdom of God is joined both to it and to everything else that is in it; that is to say, the Kingdom of God is orderly. A third principle is that humans do not and can never know either all the creatures that the Kingdom of God contains or the whole pattern or order by which it contains them.

The suitability of the Kingdom of God as, so to speak, a place name is partly owing to the fact that it still means pretty much what it has always meant. Because, I think, of the embarrassment that the phrase has increasingly caused among the educated, it has not been much tainted or tampered with by the disinterested processes of academic thought; it is a phrase that comes to us with its cultural strings still attached. To say that we live in the Kingdom of God is both to suggest the difficulty of our condition and to imply a fairly complete set of culture-borne instructions for living in it. These instructions are not always explicitly eco-logical, but it can be argued that they are always implicitly so, for all of them rest ultimately on the assumptions that I have given as the second and third principles of the Kingdom of God: that we live within order and that this order is both greater and more intricate than we can know. The difficulty of our predicament, then, is made clear if we add a fourth principle: Though we cannot produce a complete or even an adequate description of this order, severe penalties are in store for us if we presume upon it or violate it.

I am not dealing, of course, with perceptions that are only Biblical. The ancient Greeks, according to Aubrey de Sélincourt, saw "a continuing moral pattern in the vicissitudes of human fortune," a pattern "formed from the belief that men, as men, are subject to certain limitations imposed by a Power—call it Fate or God—which they cannot fully comprehend, and that any attempt to transcend those limitations is met by inevitable punishment."[1] The Greek name for the pride that attempts to transcend human limitations was *hubris,* and hubris was the cause of what the Greeks understood as tragedy.

Nearly the same sense of *necessary* human limitation is implied in the Old Testament's repeated remonstrances against too great a human confidence in the power of "mine own hand." Gideon's army against the Midianites, for example, was reduced from thirty-two thousand to three hundred expressly to prevent the Israelites from saying, "Mine own hand hath saved me."[2] A similar purpose was served by the institution of the Sabbath, when, by not working, the Israelites were meant to see the limited efficacy of their work and thus to understand their true dependence.

Though I hope that my insistence on the usefulness of the term, the Kingdom of God, will be understood, I must acknowledge that the term is local, in the sense that it is fully available only to those whose languages are involved in Western or Biblical tradition. A person of Eastern heritage, for example, might speak of the totality of all creation, visible and invisible, as "the Tao." I am well aware also that many people would not willingly use either term, or any such term. For these reasons, I do not want to make a statement that is specially or exclusively Biblical, and so I would like now to introduce a more culturally neutral term for that economy that I have been calling the Kingdom of God. Sometimes, in thinking about it, I have called it the Great Economy, which is the name I am going to make do with here—though I will remain under the personal necessity of Biblical reference. And that, I think, must be one of my points: We can name it whatever we wish, but we cannot define it except by way of a religious tradition. The Great Economy, like the Tao or the Kingdom of God, is both known and unknown, visible and invisible, comprehensible and mysterious. It is, thus, the ultimate condition of our experience and of the practical questions rising from our experience, and it imposes on our consideration of those questions an extremity of seriousness and an extremity of humility.

I am assuming that the Great Economy, whatever we may name it, is indeed—and in ways that are, to some extent, practical—an economy: It includes principles and patterns by which values or powers or necessities are parceled out and exchanged. But if the Great Economy comprehends humans and thus cannot be fully comprehended by them, then it is also not an economy in which humans can participate directly. What this suggests, in fact, is that humans can live in the Great Economy only with great uneasiness, subject to powers and laws that they can understand only in part. There is no human accounting for the Great Economy. This obviously is a description of the circumstance of religion, the circumstance that *causes* religion. De Sélincourt states the problem succinctly: "Religion in every age is concerned with the vast and fluctuant regions of experience which knowledge cannot penetrate, the regions which a man knows, or feels, to stretch away beyond the narrow, closed circle of what he can *manage* by the use of his wits."[3]

If there is no denying our dependence on the Great Economy, there is also no denying our need for a little economy—a narrow circle within which things are manageable by the use of our wits. I don't think Wes Jackson was denying this need when he invoked the Kingdom of God as the complete economy; rather, he was, I think, insisting upon a priority that is both proper and practical. If he had a text in mind, it must have been the sixth chapter of Matthew, in which, after speaking of God's care for nature, the fowls of the air and the lilies of the field, Jesus says: "Therefore take no thought, saying, What shall we eat? or, What shall we drink? or, Wherewithal shall we be clothed? . . . But seek ye first the kingdom of God, and his righteousness; and all these things shall be added unto you."[4]

There is an attitude that sees in this text a denial of the value of *any* economy of this world, but this attitude makes the text useless and meaningless to humans who must live in this world. These verses make usable sense only if we read them as a statement of considerable practical import about the real nature of worldly economy. If this passage meant for us to seek *only* the Kingdom of God, it would have the odd result of making good people not only feckless but also dependent upon bad people busy with quite other seekings. It says, rather, to seek the Kingdom of God *first;* that is, it gives an obviously necessary priority to the Great Economy over any little economy made within it. The passage also clearly includes nature within the Great Economy, and it affirms the goodness, indeed the sanctity, of natural creatures.

The fowls of the air and the lilies of the field live within the Great Economy entirely by nature, whereas humans, though entirely dependent upon it, must live in it partly by artifice. The birds can live in the Great Economy only as birds, the flowers only as flowers, the humans only as humans. The humans, unlike the wild creatures, may choose not to live in it—or, rather, since no creature can escape it, they may choose to *act* as if they do not, or they may choose to try to live in it on their own terms. If humans choose to live in the Great Economy on *its* terms, then they must live in harmony with it, maintaining it in trust and learning to consider the lives of the wild creatures.

Certain economic restrictions are clearly implied, and these restrictions have mainly to do with the economics of futurity. We know from other passages in the Gospels that a certain preparedness or provisioning for the future is required of us. It may be that such preparedness is part of our obligation to today, and for *that* reason we need "take no thought for the morrow."[5] But it is clear that such preparations can be carried too far, that we can provide too much for the future. The sin of "a certain rich man" in the twelfth chapter of Luke is that he has "much goods laid up for many years" and thus believes that he can "eat, drink, and be merry."[6] The offense seems to be that he has stored up too much and in the process has belittled the future, for he has reduced it to the size of his own hopes and expectations. He is prepared for a future in which he will be prosperous, not for one in which he will be dead. We know from our own experience that it is possible to live in the present in such a way as to diminish the future practically as well as spiritually. By laying up "much goods" in the present—and, in the process, *using up* such goods as topsoil, fossil fuel, and fossil water—we incur a debt to the future that we cannot repay. That is, we diminish the future by deeds that we call "use" but that the future will call "theft." We may say, then, that we seek the Kingdom of God, in part, by our economic behavior, and we fail to find it if that behavior is wrong.

If we read Matthew 6:24–34 as a teaching that is *both* practical and spiritual, as I think we must, then we must see it as prescribing the terms of a kind of little economy or human economy. Since I am deriving it here from a Christian text, we could call it a Christian economy. But we need not call it that. A Buddhist might look at the working principles of the economy I am talking about and call it a Buddhist economy. E. F. Schumacher, in fact, says that the aim of "Buddhist economics" is "to obtain the maximum of well-being with the minimum of consumption,"[7] which I think is partly the sense of Matthew 6:24–34. Or we could call this economy (from Matthew 6:28) a "considerate" economy or, simply, a good economy. Whatever the name, the human economy, if it is to be a good economy, must fit harmoniously within and must correspond to the Great Economy; in certain important ways, it must be an analogue of the Great Economy.

A fifth principle of the Great Economy that must now be added to the previous four is that *we* cannot foresee an end to it: The same basic stuff is going to be shifting from one form to another, so far as we know, forever. From a human point of view, this is a rather heartless endurance. As cynics sometimes point out, conservation is always working, for what is lost or wasted in one place always turns up someplace else. Thus, soil erosion in Iowa involves no loss because the soil is conserved in the Gulf of Mexico. Such people like to point out that soil erosion is as "natural" as birdsong. And so it is, though these people neglect to observe that soil conservation is also natural, and that, before the advent of farming, nature alone worked effectively to keep Iowa topsoil in Iowa. But to say that soil erosion is natural is only a way of saying that there are some things that the Great Economy cannot do for humans. Only a little economy, only a good human economy, can define for us the value of keeping the topsoil where it is.

A good human economy, that is, defines and values human goods, and, like the Great Economy, it conserves and protects its goods. It proposes to endure. Like the Great Economy, a good human economy does not propose for itself a term to be set by humans. That termlessness, with all its implied human limits and restraints, is a human good.

The difference between the Great Economy and any human economy is pretty much the difference between the goose that laid the golden egg and the golden egg. For the goose to have value as a layer of golden eggs, she must be a live goose and therefore joined to the life cycle, which means that she is joined to all manner of things, patterns, and processes that sooner or later surpass human comprehension. The golden egg, on the other hand, can be fully valued by humans according to kind, weight, and measure—but it will not hatch, and it cannot be eaten. To make the value of the egg *fully* accountable, then, we must make it "golden," must remove it from life. But if in our valuation of it, we wish to consider its relation to the goose, we have to undertake a different kind of accounting, more exacting if less exact. That is, if we wish to value the egg in such a way as to preserve the goose that laid it, we find that we must behave, not scientifically, but humanely; we must understand ourselves as humans as fully as our traditional knowledge of ourselves permits. We participate in our little human economy to a considerable extent, that is, by factual knowledge, calculation, and manipulation; our participation in the Great Economy also requires those things, but requires as well humility, sympathy, forbearance, generosity, imagination.

Another critical difference, implicit in the foregoing, is that, though a human economy can evaluate, distribute, use, and preserve things of value, it cannot make value. Value can originate only in the Great Economy. It is true enough that humans can add value to natural things: We may transform trees into boards, and transform boards into chairs, adding value at each transformation. In a good human economy, these transformations would be made by good work, which would be properly valued and the workers properly rewarded. But a good human economy would recognize at the same time that it was dealing all along with materials and powers that it did not make. It did not make trees, and it did not make the intelligence and talents of the human workers. What the humans have added at every step is artificial, made by art, and though the value of art is critical to human life, it is a secondary value.

When humans presume to originate value, they make value that is first abstract and then false, tyrannical, and destructive of real value. Money value, for instance, can be said to be true only when it justly and stably represents the value of necessary goods, such as clothing, food, and shelter, which originate ultimately in the Great Economy. Humans can originate money value in the abstract, but only by inflation and usury, which falsify the value of necessary things and damage their natural and human sources. Inflation and usury and the damages that follow can be understood, perhaps, as retributions for the presumption that humans can make value.

We may say, then, that a human economy originates, manages, and distributes secondary or added values but that, if it is to last long, it must also manage in such a way as to make continuously available those values that are primary or given, the secondary values having mainly to do with husbandry and trusteeship. A little economy is obliged to receive them gratefully and to use them in such a way as not to diminish them. We might make a long list of things that we would have to describe as primary values, which come directly into the little economy from the Great, but the one I want to talk about, because it is the one with which we have the most intimate working relationship, is the topsoil.

We cannot speak of topsoil, indeed we cannot know what it is, without acknowledging at the outset that we cannot make it. We can care for it (or not), we can even, as we say, "build" it, but we can do so only by assenting to, preserving, and perhaps collaborating in its own processes. To those processes themselves we have nothing to contribute. We cannot make topsoil, and we cannot make any substitute for it; we cannot do what it does. It is apparently impossible to make an adequate description of topsoil in the sort of language that we have come to call "scientific." For, although any soil sample can be reduced to its inert quantities, a handful of the real thing has life in it; it is full of living creatures. And if we try to describe the behavior of that life we will see that it is doing something that, if we are not careful, we will call "unearthly": It is making life out of death. Not so very long ago, had we known about it what we know now, we would probably have called it "miraculous." In a time when death is looked upon with almost universal enmity, it is hard to believe that the land we live on and the lives we live are the gifts of death. Yet that is so, and it is the topsoil that makes it so. In fact, in talking about topsoil, it is hard to avoid the language of religion. When, in "This Compost," Whitman says, "The resurrection of the wheat appears with pale visage out of its graves," he is speaking in the Christian tradition, and yet he is describing what happens, with language that is entirely accurate and appropriate. And when at last he says of the earth that "It gives such divine materials to men," we feel that the propriety of the words comes not from convention but from the actuality of the uncanny transformation that his poem has required us to imagine, as if in obedience to the summons to "consider the lilies of the field."

Even in its functions that may seem, to mechanists, to be mechanical, the topsoil behaves complexly and wonderfully. A healthy topsoil, for instance, has at once the ability to hold water and to drain well. When we speak of the health of a watershed, these abilities are what we are talking about, and the word "health," which we do use in speaking of watersheds, warns us that we are not speaking merely of mechanics. A healthy soil is made by the life dying into it and by the life living in it, and to its double ability to drain and retain water we are complexly indebted, for it not only gives us good crops but also erosion control as well as *both* flood control and a constant water supply.

Obviously, topsoil, not energy or money, is the critical quantity in agriculture. And topsoil *is* a quantity; we need it in quantities. We now need more of it than we have; we need to help it to make more of itself. But it is a most peculiar quantity, for it is inseparable from quality. Topsoil is by definition *good* soil, and it can be preserved in human use only by good care. When humans see it as a mere quantity, they tend to make it that; they destroy the life in it, and they begin to measure in inches and feet and tons how much of it they have "lost."

When we see the topsoil as the foundation of that household of living creatures and their nonliving supports that we now call an "ecosystem" but which some of us understand better as a "neighborhood," we find ourselves in debt for other benefits that baffle our mechanical logic and defy our measures. For example, one of the principles of an ecosystem is that diversity increases capacity—or, to put it another way, that complications of form or pattern can increase greatly within quantitative limits. I suppose that this may be true only up to a point, but I suppose also that that point is far beyond the human capacity to understand or diagram the pattern.

On a farm put together on a sound ecological pattern, the same principle holds. Henry Besuden, the great farmer and shepherd of Clark County, Kentucky, compares the small sheep flock to the two spoons of sugar that can be added to a brimful cup of coffee, which then becomes "more palatable [but] doesn't run over. You can stock your farm to the limit with other livestock and still add a small flock of sheep." He says this, characteristically, after rejecting the efforts of sheep specialists to get beyond "the natural physical limits of the ewe" by breeding out of season in order to get three lamb crops in two years or by striving for "litters" of lambs rather than nature's optimum of twins. Rather than chafe at "natural physical limits," he would turn to nature's elegant way of enriching herself *within* her physical limits by diversification, by complication of pattern. Rather than strain the productive capacity of the ewe, he would, without strain, enlarge the productive capacity of the farm—a healthier, safer, and cheaper procedure. Like many of the better traditional farmers, Henry Besuden is suspicious of "the measure of land in length and width," for he would be mindful as well of "the depth and quality."[8]

A small flock of ewes, fitted properly into a farm's pattern, virtually disappears into the farm and does it good, just as it virtually disappears into the time and energy economy of a farm family and does it good. And, properly fitted into the farm's pattern, the small flock virtually disappears from the debit side of the farm's accounts but shows up plainly on the credit side. This "disappearance" is possible, not to the extent that the farm is a human artifact, a belonging of the human economy, but to the extent that it remains, by its obedience to natural principle, a belonging of the Great Economy.

A little economy may be said to be good insofar as it perceives the excellence of these benefits and husbands and preserves them. It is by holding up this standard of goodness that we can best see what is wrong with the industrial economy. For the industrial economy does not see itself as a little economy; it sees itself as the *only* economy. It makes itself thus exclusive by the simple expedient of valuing only what it can use—that is, only what it can regard as "raw material" to be transformed mechanically into something else. What it cannot use, it characteristically describes as "useless," "worthless," "random," or "wild," and gives it some such name as "chaos," "disorder," or "waste"—and thus ruins it or cheapens it in preparation for eventual use. That western deserts or eastern mountains were once perceived as "useless" made it easy to dignify them by the "use" of strip mining. Once we acknowledge the existence of the Great Economy, however, we are astonished and frightened to see how much modern enterprise is the work of hubris, occurring outside the human boundary established by ancient tradition. The industrial economy is based on invasion and pillage of the Great Economy.

The weakness of the industrial economy is clearly revealed when it imposes its terms upon agriculture, for its terms cannot define those natural principles that are most vital to the life and longevity of farms. Even if the industrial economists could afford to do so, they could not describe the dependence of agriculture upon nature. If asked to consider the lilies of the field or told that the wheat is resurrected out of its graves, the agricultural industrialist would reply that "my engineer's mind inclines less toward the poetic and philosophical, and more toward the practical and possible,"[9] unable even to suspect that such a division of mind induces blindness to possibilities of the utmost practical concern.

That good topsoil both drains and retains water, that diversity increases capacity, are facts similarly alien to industrial logic. Industrialists see retention and drainage as different and opposite functions, and they would promote one at the expense of the other, just as, diversity being inimical to industrial procedure, they would commit themselves to the forlorn expedient of enlarging capacity by increasing area. They are thus encumbered by dependence on mechanical solutions that can work only by isolating and oversimplifying problems. Industrialists are condemned to proceed by devices. To facilitate water retention, they must resort to a specialized water-holding device such as a terrace or a dam; to facilitate drainage, they must use drain tile, or a ditch, or a "subsoiler." It is possible, I know, to argue that this analysis is too general and to produce exceptions, but I do not think it deniable that the discipline of soil conservation is now principally that of the engineer, not that of the farmer or soil husband—that it is now a matter of digging in the earth, not of enriching it.

I do not mean to say that the devices of engineering are always inappropriate; they have their place, not least in the restoration of land abused by the devices of engineering. My point is that, to facilitate both water retention and drainage in the same place, we must improve the soil, which is not a mechanical device but, among other things, a graveyard, a place of resurrection, and a community of living creatures. Devices may sometimes help, but only up to a point, for soil is improved by what humans do not do as well as by what they do. The proprieties of soil husbandry require acts that are much more complex than industrial acts, for these acts are conditioned by the ability *not* to act, by forbearance or self-restraint, sympathy or generosity. The industrial act is simply prescribed by thought, but the act of soil building is also *limited* by thought. We build soil by knowing what to do but also by knowing what not to do and by knowing when to stop. Both kinds of knowledge are necessary because invariably, at some point, the reach of human comprehension becomes too short, and at that point the work of the human economy must end in absolute deference to the working of the Great Economy. This, I take it, is the practical significance of the idea of the Sabbath.

To push our work beyond that point, invading the Great Economy, is to become guilty of hubris, of presuming to be greater than we are. We cannot do what the topsoil does, any more than we can do what God does or what a swallow does. We can fly, but only as humans—very crudely, noisily, and clumsily. We can dispose of corpses and garbage, but we cannot, by our devices, turn them into fertility and new life. And we are discovering, to our great uneasiness, that we cannot dispose at all of some of our so-called wastes that are toxic or radioactive. We can appropriate and in some fashion use godly powers, but we cannot use them safely, and we cannot control the results. That is to say that the human condition remains for us what it was for Homer and the authors of the Bible. Now that we have brought such enormous powers to our aid (we hope), it seems more necessary than ever to observe how inexorably the human condition still contains us. We only do what humans can do, and our machines, however they may appear to enlarge our possibilities, are invariably infected with our limitations. Sometimes, in enlarging our possibilities, they narrow our limits and leave us more powerful but less content, less safe, and less free. The mechanical means by which we propose to escape the human condition only extend it; thinking to transcend our definition as fallen creatures, we have only colonized more and more territory eastward of Eden.

II

Like the rich man of the parable, the industrialist thinks to escape the persistent obligations of the human condition by means of "much goods laid up for many years"—by means, in other words, of quantities: resources, supplies, stockpiles, funds, reserves. But this is a grossly oversimplifying dream and, thus, a dangerous one. All the great natural goods that empower agriculture, some of which I have discussed, have to do with quantities, but they have to do also with qualities, and they involve principles that are not static but active; they have to do with formal processes. The topsoil exists as such because it is ceaselessly transforming death into life, ceaselessly supplying food and water to all that lives in it and from it; otherwise, "All flesh shall perish together, and man shall turn again unto dust"[10]. If we are to live well on and from our land, we must live by faith in the ceaselessness of these processes and by faith in our own willingness and ability to collaborate with them. Christ's prayer for "daily bread" is an affirmation of such faith, just as it is a repudiation of faith in "much goods laid up." Our life and liveli-

hood are the gift of the topsoil and of our willingness and ability
to care for it, to grow good wheat, to make good bread; they do
not derive from stockpiles of raw materials or accumulations of
purchasing power.

The industrial economy can define potentiality, even the potentiality of the living topsoil, only as a *fund,* and thus it must
accept impoverishment as the inescapable condition of abundance. The invariable mode of its relation both to nature and to
human culture is that of mining: withdrawal from a limited fund
until that fund is exhausted. It removes natural fertility and human workmanship from the land, just as it removes nourishment
and human workmanship from bread. Thus the land is reduced
to abstract marketable quantities of length and width, and bread
to merchandise that is high in money value but low in food value.
"Our bread," Guy Davenport once said to me, "is more obscene
than our movies."

But the industrial use of *any* "resource" implies its exhaustion.
It is for this reason that the industrial economy has been accompanied by an ever-increasing hurry of research and exploration,
the motive of which is not "free enterprise" or "the spirit of free
inquiry," as industrial scientists and apologists would have us
believe, but the desperation that naturally and logically accom-
panies gluttony.

One of the favorite words of the industrial economy is "control": We want "to keep things under control"; we wish (or so we
say) to "control" inflation and erosion; we have a discipline known
as "crowd control"; we believe in "controlled growth" and "controlled development," in "traffic control" and "self-control." But,
because we are always setting out to control something that we
refuse to limit, we have made control a permanent and a helpless
enterprise. If we will not limit causes, there can be no controlling
of effects. What is to be the fate of self-control in an economy that
encourages and rewards unlimited selfishness?

More than anything else, we would like to "control the forces
of nature," refusing at the same time to impose any limit on

human nature. We assume that such control and such freedom are our "rights," which seems to ensure that our means of control (of nature and of all else that we see as alien) will be violent. It is startling to recognize the extent to which the industrial economy depends upon controlled explosions—in mines, in weapons, in the cylinders of engines, in the economic pattern known as "boom and bust." This dependence is the result of a progress that can be argued for, but those who argue for it must recognize that, in all these means, good ends are served by a destructive principle, an association that is difficult to control if it is not limited; moreover, they must recognize that our failure to limit this association has raised the specter of uncontrollable explosion. Nuclear holocaust, if it comes, will be the final detonation of an explosive economy.

An explosive economy, then, is not only an economy that is dependent upon explosions but also one that sets no limits on itself. Any little economy that sees itself as unlimited is obviously self-blinded. It does not see its real relation of dependence and obligation to the Great Economy; in fact, it does not see that there *is* a Great Economy. Instead, it calls the Great Economy "raw material" or "natural resources" or "nature" and proceeds with the business of putting it "under control."

But "control" is a word more than ordinarily revealing here, for its root meaning is to roll against, in the sense of a little wheel turning in opposition. The principle of control, then, involves necessarily the principle of division: One thing may turn against another thing only by being divided from it. This mechanical division and turning in opposition William Blake understood as evil, and he spoke of "Satanic wheels" and "Satanic mills": "wheel without wheel, with cogs tyrannic / Moving by compulsion each other."[11] By "wheel without wheel," Blake meant wheel outside of wheel, one wheel communicating motion to the other in the manner of two cogwheels, the point being that one wheel can turn another wheel outside itself only in a direction opposite to its own. This, I suppose, is acceptable enough as a mechanism. It becomes "Satanic" when it becomes a ruling metaphor and is used to describe and to organize fundamental relationships. Against the Satanic "wheel without wheel," Blake set the wheels of Eden, which "Wheel within wheel in freedom revolve, in harmony and peace."[12] This is the "wheel in the middle of a wheel"[13] of Ezekiel's vision, and it is an image of harmony. That the relation of these wheels is not mechanical we know from Ezekiel 1:21: "the spirit of the living creature was in the wheels." The wheels of opposition oppose the spirit of the living creature.

What had happened, as Blake saw accurately and feared justifiably, was a fundamental shift in the relation of humankind to the rest of creation. Sometime between, say, Pope's verses on the Chain of Being in *An Essay on Man* and Blake's "London," the dominant minds had begun to see the human race, not as a part or a member of Creation, but as outside it and opposed to it. The industrial revolution was only a part of this change, but it is true that, when the wheels of the industrial revolution began to revolve, they turned against nature, which became the name for all of Creation thought to be below humanity, as well as, incidentally, against all once thought to be above humanity. Perhaps this would have been safe enough if nature—that is, if all the rest of Creation—had been, as proposed, passively subject to human purpose.

Of course, it never has been. As Blake foresaw, and as we now know, what we turn against must turn against us. Blake's image of the cogwheels turning in relentless opposition is terrifyingly apt, for in our vaunted war against nature, nature fights back. The earth may answer our pinches and pokes "only with spring,"[14] as e. e. cummings said, but if we pinch and poke too much, she can answer also with flood or drouth, with catastrophic soil erosion, with plague and famine. Many of the occurrences that we call "acts of God" or "accidents of nature" are simply forthright natural responses to human provocations. Not always; I do not mean to imply here that, by living in harmony with nature, we can be free of floods and storms and drouths and earth-quakes and volcanic eruptions; I am only pointing out, as many others have done, that, by living in opposition to nature, we can *cause* natural calamities of which we would otherwise be free.

The problem seems to be that a human economy cannot pre-scribe the terms of its own success. In a time when we wish to believe that humans are the sole authors of the truth, that truth is relative, and that value judgments are all subjective, it is hard to say that a human economy can be wrong, and yet we have good, sound, practical reasons for saying so. It is indeed possible for a human economy to be wrong—not relatively wrong, in the sense of being "out of adjustment," or unfair according to some human definition of fairness, or weak according to the definition of its own purposes—but wrong absolutely and according to practical measures. Of course, if we see the human economy as the *only* economy, we will see its errors as political failures, and we will continue to talk about "recovery." It is only when we think of the little human economy in relation to the Great Economy that we begin to understand our errors for what they are and to see the qualitative meanings of our quantitative measures. If we see the industrial economy in terms of the Great Economy, then we begin to see industrial wastes and losses not as "trade-offs" or "neces-sary risks" but as costs that, like all costs, are chargeable to somebody, sometime.

That we can prescribe the terms of our own success, that we can live outside or in ignorance of the Great Economy are the greatest errors. They condemn us to a life without a standard, wavering in inescapable bewilderment from paltry self-satisfac-tion to paltry self-dissatisfaction. But since we have no place to live but in the Great Economy, whether or not we know that and act accordingly is the critical question, not about economy mere-ly, but about human life itself.

It is possible to make a little economy, such as our present one, that is so short-sighted and in which accounting is of so short a term as to give the impression that vices are necessary and practically justifiable. When we make our economy a little wheel turning in opposition to what we call "nature," then we set up competitiveness as the ruling principle in our explanation of reality and in our understanding of economy; we make of it, willy-nilly, a virtue. But competitiveness, as a ruling principle and a virtue, imposes a logic that is extremely difficult, perhaps impossible, to control. That logic explains why our cars and our clothes are shoddily made, why our "wastes" are toxic, and why our "defensive" weapons are suicidal; it explains why it is so difficult for us to draw a line between "free enterprise" and crime. If our economic ideal is maximum profit with minimum responsibility, why should we be surprised to find our corporations so frequently in court and robbery on the increase? Why should we be surprised to find that medicine has become an exploitive industry, profitable in direct proportion to its hurry and its mechanical indifference? People who pay for shoddy products or careless services and people who are robbed outright are equally victims of theft, the only difference being that the robbers outright are not guilty of fraud.

If, on the other hand, we see ourselves as living within the Great Economy, under the necessity of making our little human economy within it, according to its terms, the smaller wheel turning in sympathy with the greater, receiving its being and its motion from it, then we see that the traditional virtues are necessary and are practically justifiable. Then, because in the Great Economy *all* transactions count and the account is never "closed," the ideal changes. We see that we cannot *afford* maximum profit or power with minimum responsibility because, in the Great Economy, the loser's losses finally afflict the winner. Now the ideal must be "the maximum of well-being with the minimum of consumption," which both defines and requires neighborly love. Competitiveness cannot be the ruling principle, for the Great Economy is not a "side" that we can join nor are there such "sides" within it. Thus, it is not the "sum of its parts" but a *membership* of parts inextricably joined to each other, indebted to each other, receiving significance and worth from each other and from the whole. One is obliged to "consider the lilies of the field," not because they are lilies or because they are exemplary, but because they are fellow members and because, as fellow members, we and the lilies are in certain critical ways alike.

To say that within the Great Economy the virtues are necessary and practically justifiable is at once to remove them from that specialized, sanctimonious, condescending practice of virtuousness that is humorless, pointless, and intolerable to its beneficiaries. For a human, the good choice in the Great Economy is to see its membership as a neighborhood and oneself as a neighbor within it. I am sure that virtues count in a neighborhood—to "love thy neighbor as thyself" requires the help of all seven of them—but I am equally sure that in a neighborhood the virtues cannot be practiced as such. Temperance has no appearance or action of its own, nor does justice, prudence, fortitude, faith, hope, or charity. They can only be employed on occasions. "He who would do good to another," William Blake said, "must do it in Minute Particulars."[15] To help each other, that is, we must go beyond the coldhearted charity of the "general good" and get down to work where we are:

> Labour well the Minute Particulars, attend to the Little-ones,
> And those who are in misery cannot remain so long
> If we do but our duty: labour well the teeming Earth.[16]

It is the Great Economy, not any little economy, that invests minute particulars with high and final importance. In the Great Economy, each part stands for the whole and is joined to it; the whole is present in the part and is its health. The industrial economy, by contrast, is always striving and failing to make fragments (pieces that *it* has broken) *add up* to an ever-fugitive wholeness.

Work that is authentically placed and understood within the Great Economy moves virtue toward virtuosity—that is, toward skill or technical competence. There is no use in helping our

neighbors with their work if we do not know how to work. When
the virtues are rightly practiced within the Great Economy, we
do not call them virtues; we call them good farming, good forestry, good carpentry, good husbandry, good weaving and sew-
ing, good homemaking, good parenthood, good neighborhood,
and so on. The general principles are submerged in the particu-
larities of their engagement with the world. Lao Tzu saw the
appearance of the virtues as such, in the abstract, as indicative of
their loss:

> When people lost sight of the way to live
> Came codes of love and honesty . . .
> When differences weakened family ties
> Came benevolent fathers and dutiful sons;
> And when lands were disrupted and misgoverned
> Came ministers commended as loyal.[17]

And these lines might be read as an elaboration of the warning
against the *appearances* of goodness at the beginning of the sixth
chapter of Matthew.

The work of the small economy, when it is understandingly
placed within the Great Economy, minutely particularizes the
virtues and carries principle into practice; to the extent that it
does so, it escapes specialization. The industrial economy requires the extreme specialization of work—the separation of
work from its results—because it subsists upon divisions of interest and must deny the fundamental kinships of producer and
consumer; seller and buyer; owner and worker; worker, work,
and product; parent material and product; nature and artifice;
thoughts, words, and deeds. Divided from those kinships, specialized artists and scientists identify themselves as "observers"
or "objective observers"—that is, as outsiders without responsibility or involvement. But the industrialized arts and sciences
are false, their division is a lie, for there is no specialization of
results.

There is no "outside" to the Great Economy, no escape into
either specialization or generality, no "time off." Even insignifi-

cance is no escape, for in the membership of the Great Economy everything signifies; whatever we do counts. If we do not serve what coheres and endures, we serve what disintegrates and destroys. We can *presume* that we are outside the membership that includes us, but that presumption only damages the membership—and ourselves, of course, along with it.

In the industrial economy, the arts and the sciences are specialized "professions," each having its own language, speaking to none of the others. But the Great Economy proposes arts and sciences of membership: ways of doing and ways of knowing that cannot be divided from each other or within themselves and that speak the common language of the communities where they are practiced.

NOTES

1. Aubrey de Sélincourt, *The World of Herodotus* (San Francisco: North Point Press, 1982), p. 23.
2. Judges 7:2–21.
3. Sélincourt, *World of Herodotus*, p. 171.
4. Matt. 6:31, 33.
5. Matt. 6:34.
6. Luke 12:16–19.
7. E. F. Schumacher, *Small is Beautiful* (New York: Harper & Row, 1973) p. 54.
8. Henry Besuden, Speech delivered to International Stockmen's School, San Antonio, Texas, January 2–6, 1983.
9. Gordon Millar, "Agriculture: Is Small Really Beautiful?," *World Research INK* (January 1978), p. 10.
10. Job 34:15
11. William Blake, *Jerusalem,* plate 15, lines 18–19.
12. Ibid., line 20.
13. Ezek. 1:16.
14. e.e. cummings, *Poems 1923–1954* (New York: Harcourt, Brace and Company, 1954), p. 39.
15. Blake, *Jerusalem,* plate 55, line 60.
16. Ibid., lines 51–53.
17. Lao Tzu, *The Way of Life (Tao Teh Ching),* trans. Witter Bynner (New York: Capricorn Books, 1962), p. 35.

The Loss
of the University

1984

The predicament of literature within the university is not fundamentally different from the predicament of any other discipline, which is not fundamentally different from the predicament of language. That is, the various disciplines have ceased to speak to each other; they have become too specialized, and this over-specialization, this separation, of the disciplines has been enabled and enforced by the specialization of their languages. As a result, the modern university has grown, not according to any unifying principle, like an expanding universe, but according to the principle of miscellaneous accretion, like a furniture storage business.

I assume that there is a degree of specialization that is unavoidable because concentration involves a narrowing of attention; we can only do one thing at a time. I assume further that there is a degree of specialization that is desirable because good work depends upon sustained practice. If we want the best work to be done in teaching or writing or stone masonry or farming, then we must arrange for that work to be done by proven master workers, people who are prepared for the work by long and excellent practice.

But to assume that there is a degree of specialization that is proper is at the same time to assume that there is a degree that is improper. The impropriety begins, I think, when the various kinds of workers come to be divided and cease to speak to one another. In this division they become makers of *parts* of things. This is the impropriety of industrial organization, of which Eric Gill wrote, "Skill in making . . . degenerates into mere dexterity, i.e. skill in doing, when the workman . . . ceases to be concerned for the thing made or . . . has no longer any responsibility for the thing made and has therefore lost the knowledge of what it is that he is making. . . . The factory hand can only know what he is *doing*. What is being made is no concern of his."[1] Part of the problem in universities now (or part of the cause of the problem) is this loss of concern for the thing made and, back of that, I think, the loss of agreement on what the thing is that is being made.

The thing being made in a university is humanity. Given the current influence of universities, this is merely inevitable. But what universities, at least the public-supported ones, are *mandated* to make or to help to make is human beings in the fullest sense of those words—not just trained workers or knowledgeable citizens but responsible heirs and members of human culture. If the proper work of the university is only to equip people to fulfill private ambitions, then how do we justify public support? If it is only to prepare citizens to fulfill public responsibilities, then how do we justify the teaching of arts and sciences? The common denominator has to be larger than either career preparation or preparation for citizenship. Underlying the idea of a university— the bringing together, the combining into one, of all the disciplines—is the idea that good work and good citizenship are the inevitable by-products of the making of a good—that is, a fully developed—human being. This, as I understand it, is the definition of the name *university*.

In order to be concerned for the thing made, in order even to know what it is making, the university as a whole must speak the same language as all of its students and all of its graduates. There must, in other words, be a common tongue. Without a common tongue, a university not only loses concern for the thing made; it loses its own unity. Furthermore, when the departments of a university become so specialized that they can speak neither to each other nor to the students and graduates of other departments, then that university is displaced. As an institution, it no longer knows where it is, and therefore it cannot know either its responsibilities to its place or the effects of its irresponsibility. This too often is the practical meaning of "academic freedom": The teacher feels free to teach and learn, make and think, without concern for the thing made.

For example, it is still perfectly acceptable in land-grant universities for agricultural researchers to apply themselves to the development of more productive dairy cows without considering at all the fact that this development necessarily involves the failure of many thousands of dairies and dairy farmers—that it has already done so and will inevitably continue to do so. The researcher feels at liberty to justify such work merely on the basis of the ratio between the "production unit" and the volume of production. And such work is permitted to continue, I suspect, because it is reported in language that is unreadable and probably unintelligible to nearly everybody in the university, to nearly everybody who milks cows, and to nearly everybody who drinks milk. That a modern university might provide a forum in which such researchers might be required to defend their work before colleagues in, say, philosophy or history or literature is, at present, not likely, nor is it likely, at present, that the departments of philosophy, history, or literature could produce many colleagues able or willing to be interested in the ethics of agricultural research.

Language is at the heart of the problem. To profess, after all, is "to confess before"—to confess, I assume, before all who live within the neighborhood or under the influence of the confessor. But to confess before one's neighbors and clients in a language that few of them can understand is not to confess at all. The specialized professional language is thus not merely a contradiction in terms; it is a cheat and a hiding place; it may, indeed, be an ambush. At the very root of the idea of profession and professorship is the imperative to speak plainly in the common tongue.

That the common tongue should become the exclusive specialty of a department in a university is therefore a tragedy, and not just for the university and its worldly place; it is a tragedy for the common tongue. It means that the common tongue, so far as the university is concerned, *ceases* to be the common tongue; it becomes merely one tongue within a confusion of tongues. Our language and literature cease to be seen as occurring in the world, and begin to be seen as occurring within their university department and within themselves. Literature ceases to be the meeting ground of all readers of the common tongue and becomes only the occasion of a deafening clatter *about* literature. Teachers and students read the great songs and stories to learn *about* them, not to learn *from* them. The *texts* are tracked as by the passing of an army of ants, but the power of songs and stories to affect life is still little acknowledged, apparently because it is little felt.

The specialist approach, of course, is partly justifiable; in both speech and literature, language does occur within itself. It echoes within itself, reverberating endlessly like a voice echoing within a cave, and speaking in answer to its echo, and the answer again echoing. It must do this; its nature, in part, is to do this.

But its nature also is to turn outward to the world, to strike its worldly objects cleanly and cease to echo—to achieve a kind of rest and silence in them. The professionalization of language and of language study makes the cave inescapable; one strives without rest in the interior clamor.

The silence in which words return to their objects, touch them, and come to rest is not the silence of the plugged ear. It is the world's silence, such as occurs after the first hard freeze of autumn, when the weeks-long singing of the crickets is suddenly

stopped, and when, by a blessedly recurring accident, all machine noises have stopped for the moment, too. It is a silence that
must be prepared for and waited for; it requires a silence of one's
own.

The reverberations of language within itself are, finally, mere
noise, no better or worse than the noise of accumulated facts that
grate aimlessly against each other in think tanks and other hollow places. Facts, like words, are not things but verbal tokens or
signs of things that finally must be carried back to the things they
stand for to be verified. This carrying back is not specialist work
but an act generally human, though only properly humbled and
quieted humans can do it. It is an act that at once enlarges and
shapes, frees and limits us.

It is necessary, for example, that the word *tree* evoke memories
that are both personal and cultural. In order to understand fully
what a tree is, we must remember much of our experience with
trees and much that we have heard and read about them. We
destroy those memories by reducing trees to facts, by thinking of
tree as a mere word, or by treating our memory of trees as "cultural history." When we call a tree a tree, we are not isolated
among words and facts but are at once in the company of the tree
itself and surrounded by ancestral voices calling out to us all that
trees have been and meant. This is simply the condition of being
human in this world, and there is nothing that art and science can
do about it, except get used to it. But, of course, only specialized
"professional" arts and sciences would propose or wish to do
something about it.

This necessity for words and facts to return to their objects
in the world describes one of the boundaries of a university, one
of the boundaries of book learning anywhere, and it describes the
need for humility, restraint, exacting discipline, and high standards within that boundary.

Beside every effort of making, which is necessarily narrow, there
must be an effort of judgment, of criticism, which must be as
broad as possible. That is, every made thing must be submitted

to these questions: What is the quality of this thing as a human artifact, as an addition to the world of made and of created things? How suitable is it to the needs of human and natural neighborhoods?

It must, of course, sooner or later be submitted as well to the special question: How good is this poem or this farm or this hospital as such? For it to have a human value, it obviously must be well made; it must meet the specialized, technical criteria; it must be *good* as such. But the question of its quality as such is not interesting—in the long run it is probably not even askable—unless we ask it under the rule of the more general questions. If we are disposed to judge apart from the larger questions, if we judge, as well as make, as specialists, then a good forger has as valid a claim to our respect as a good artist.

These two problems, how to make and how to judge, are the business of education. But education has tended increasingly to ignore the doubleness of its obligation. It has concerned itself more and more exclusively with the problem of how to make, narrowing the issue of judgment virtually to the terms of the made thing itself. But the thing made by education now is not a fully developed human being; it is a specialist, a careerist, a graduate. In industrial education, the thing *finally* made is of no concern to the makers.

In some instances, this is because the specialized "fields" have grown so complicated within themselves that the curriculum leaves no time for the broad and basic studies that would inform judgment. In other instances, one feels that there is a potentially embarrassing conflict between judgment broadly informed and the specialized career for which the student is being prepared; teachers of advertising techniques, for example, could ill afford for their students to realize that they are learning the arts of lying and seduction. In all instances, this narrowing is justified by the improbable assumption that young students, before they know anything else, know what they need to learn.

If the disintegration of the university begins in its specialist ideology, it is enforced by a commercial compulsion to satisfy the customer. Since the student is now so much a free agent in determining his or her education, the department administrators and the faculty members must necessarily be preoccupied with the problem of how to keep enrollments up. Something obviously must be done to keep the classes filled; otherwise, the students will wander off to more attractive courses or to courses more directly useful to their proposed careers. Under such circumstances it is inevitable that requirements will be lightened, standards lowered, grades inflated, and instruction narrowed to the supposed requirements of some supposed career opportunity.

Dr. Johnson told Mrs. Thrale that his cousin, Cornelius Ford, "advised him to study the Principles of every thing, that a general Acquaintance with Life might be the Consequence of his Enquiries—Learn said he the leading Precognita of all things . . . grasp the Trunk hard only, and you will shake all the Branches."[2] The soundness of this advice seems indisputable, and the metaphor entirely apt. From the trunk it is possible to "branch out." One can begin with a trunk and develop a single branch or any number of branches; although it may be possible to begin with a branch and develop a trunk, that is neither so probable nor so promising. The modern university, at any rate, more and more resembles a loose collection of lopped branches waving about randomly in the air. "Modern knowledge is departmentalized," H. J. Massingham wrote in 1943, "while the essence of culture is initiation into wholeness, so that all the divisions of knowledge are considered as the branches of one tree, the Tree of Life whose roots went deep into earth and whose top was in heaven."[3]

This Tree, for many hundreds of years, seems to have come almost naturally to mind when we have sought to describe the form of knowledge. In Western tradition, it is at least as old as Genesis, and the form it gives us for all that we know is organic, unified, comprehensive, connective—and moral. The tree, at the beginning, was two trees: the tree of life and the tree of the knowledge of good and evil. Later, in our understanding of them, the two trees seem to have become one, or each seems to stand for the other—for in the world after the Fall, how can the two be separated? To know life is to know good and evil; to prepare young people for life is to prepare them to know the difference between good and evil. If we represent knowledge as a tree, we know that things that are divided are yet connected. We know that to observe the divisions and ignore the connections is to destroy the tree. The history of modern education may be the history of the loss of this image, and of its replacement by the pattern of the industrial machine, which subsists upon division—and by industrial economics ("publish or perish"), which is meaningless apart from division.

The need for broadly informed human judgment nevertheless remains, and this need requires inescapably an education that is broad and basic. In the face of this need, which is *both* private and public, "career preparation" is an improper use of public money, since "career preparation" serves merely private ends; it is also a waste of the student's time, since "career preparation" is best and most properly acquired in apprenticeships under the supervision of employers. The proper subject for a school, for example, is how to speak and write well, not how to be a "public speaker" or a "broadcaster" or a "creative writer" or a "technical writer" or a journalist or a practitioner of "business English." If one can speak and write well, then, given the need, one can make a speech or write an article or a story or a business letter. If one cannot speak or write well, then the tricks of a trade will be no help.

The work that should, and that can, unify a university is that of deciding what a student should be required to learn—what studies, that is, constitute the trunk of the tree of a person's education. "Career preparation," which has given so much practical support to academic specialization (and so many rewards to academic specialists) seems to have destroyed interest in this question. But the question exists and the failure to answer it (or even to ask it) imposes severe penalties on teachers, students, and the public alike. The penalties imposed on students and graduates by their failure to get a broad, basic education are, I think, obvious enough. The public penalties are also obvious if we consider, for instance, the number of certified expert speakers and writers who do not speak or write well, who do not know that they speak or write poorly, and who apparently do not care whether or not they speak or write honestly.

The penalties that this failure imposes on teachers are not so obvious, mainly, I suppose, because so far the penalties have been obscured by rewards. The penalties for teachers are the same as those for students and the public, plus one more: The failure to decide what students should be required to learn keeps the teacher from functioning as, and perhaps from becoming, a responsible adult.

There is no one to teach young people but older people, and so the older people must do it. That they do not know enough to do it, that they have never been smart enough or experienced enough or good enough to do it, does not matter. They must do it because there is no one else to do it. This is simply the elemental trial— some would say the elemental tragedy—of human life: the necessity to proceed on the basis merely of the knowledge that is available, the necessity to postpone until too late the question of the sufficiency and the truth of that knowledge.

There is, then, an inescapable component of trial and error in human education; some things that are taught will be wrong because fallible humans are the teachers. But the reason for education, its constant effort and discipline, is surely to reduce the young person's dependence on trial and error as far as possible. For it *can* be reduced. One should not have to learn everything, or the basic things, by trial and error. A child should not have to learn the danger of heat by falling into the fire. A student should not have to learn the penalties of illiteracy by being illiterate or the value of a good education by the "object lesson" of a poor one.

Teachers, moreover, are not providing "career preparation" so much as they are "preparing young people for life." This statement is not the result of educational doctrine; it is simply the fact of the matter. To prepare young people for life, teachers must dispense knowledge and enlighten ignorance, just as supposed. But ignorance is not only the affliction that teaching seeks to cure; it is also the condition, the predicament, in which teaching is done, for teachers do not know the life or the lives for which their students are being prepared.

This condition gives the lie to the claims for "career preparation," since students may not *have* the careers for which they have been prepared: The "job market" may be overfilled; the requirements for this or that career may change; the student may change, or the world may. The teacher, preparing the student for a life necessarily unknown to them both, has no excusable choice but to help the student to "grasp the Trunk."

Yet the arguments for "career preparation" continue to be made and to grow in ambition. On August 23, 1983, for example, the Associated Press announced that "the head of the Texas school board wants to require sixth-graders to choose career 'tracks' that will point them toward jobs."[4] Thus, twelve-year-old children would be "free to choose" the kind of life they wish to live. They would even be free to change "career tracks," though, according to the article, such a change would involve the penalty of a delayed graduation.

But these are free choices granted to children not prepared or ready to make them. The idea, in reality, is to impose adult choices on children, and these "choices" mask the most vicious sort of economic determinism. This idea of education as "career track" diminishes everything it touches: education, teaching, childhood, the future. And such a thing could not be contemplated for sixth-graders, obviously, if it had not already been instituted in the undergraduate programs of colleges and universities.

To require or expect or even allow young people to choose courses of study and careers that they do not yet know anything about is not, as is claimed, a grant of freedom. It is a severe limitation upon freedom. It means, in practice, that when the student has finished school and is faced then, appropriately, with the need to choose a career, he or she is prepared to choose only one. At that point, the student stands in need of a freedom of choice uselessly granted years before and forfeited in that grant.

The responsibility to decide what to teach the young is an adult responsibility. When adults transfer this responsibility to the young, whether they do it by indifference or as a grant of freedom, they trap themselves in a kind of childishness. In that failure to accept responsibility, the teacher's own learning and character are disemployed, and, in the contemporary industrialized education system, they are easily replaced by bureaucratic and methodological procedures, "job market" specifications, and tests graded by machines.

This question of what all young people should be expected to learn is now little discussed. The reason, apparently, is the tacit belief that now, with the demands of specialization so numerous and varied, such a question would be extremely hard, if not impossible, to answer. And yet this question appears to be as much within the reach of reason and common sense as any other. It cannot be denied, to begin with, that all the disciplines rest upon the knowledge of letters and the knowledge of numbers. Some rest more on letters than numbers, some more on numbers than letters, but it is surely true to say that people without knowledge of both letters and numbers are not prepared to learn much else. From there, one can proceed confidently to say that history, literature, philosophy, and foreign languages rest principally on the knowledge of letters and carry it forward, and that biology, chemistry, and physics rest on the knowledge of numbers and carry it forward. This provides us with a description of a probably adequate "core curriculum"—one that would prepare a student well both to choose a direction of further study and to go in that direction. An equally obvious need, then, is to eliminate from the curriculum all courses without content—that is, all courses in methodologies and technologies that could, and should, be learned in apprenticeships.

Besides the innate human imperfections already mentioned, other painful problems are involved in expecting and requiring students to choose the course of their own education. These problems have to do mainly with the diversity of gifts and abilities: that is, some people are not talented in some kinds of work or study; some, moreover, who are poor in one discipline may be excellent in another. Why should such people be forced into situations in which they must see themselves as poor workers or as failures?

The question is not a comfortable one, and I do not believe that it can or should be comfortably answered. There is pain in the requirement to risk failure and pain in the failure that may result from that requirement. But failure is a possibility; in varying degrees for all of us, it is inescapable. The argument for removing the possibility of failure from schoolwork is therefore necessarily specious. The wrong is not in subjecting students to the possibility of failure or in calling their failures failures; the wrong is in the teacher's inability to see that failure in school is not necessarily synonymous with and does not necessarily lead to failure in the world. The wrong is in the failure to see or respect the boundaries between the school and the world. When those are not understood and respected, then the school, the school career, the diploma are all surrounded by such a spurious and modish dignity that failure in school *is* failure in the world. It is for this reason that it is so easy to give education a money value and to sell it to consumers in job lots.

It is a fact that some people with able minds do not fit well into schools and are not properly valued by schoolish standards and tests. If such people fail in a school, their failure should be so called; a school's worth and integrity depend upon its willingness to call things by their right names. But, by the same token, a failure in school is no more than that; it does not necessarily imply or cause failure in the world, any more than it implies or causes stupidity. It is not rare for the judgment of the world to overturn the judgment of schools. There are other tests for human abilities than those given in schools, and there are some that cannot be given in schools. My own life has happened to acquaint me with several people who did not attend high school but who have been more knowledgeable in their "field" and who have had better things to say about matters of general importance than most of the doctors of philosophy I have known. This is not an "anti-intellectual" statement; it is a statement of what I take to be fact, and it means only that the uses of schools are limited— another fact, which schools prepare us to learn by surprise.

Another necessary consideration is that low expectations and standards in universities encourage the lowering of expectations and standards in the high schools and elementary schools. If the universities raise their expectations and standards, the high schools and elementary schools will raise theirs; they will have to. On the other hand, if the universities teach high school courses because the students are not prepared for university courses, then they simply relieve the high schools of their duty and in the process make themselves unable to do their own duty. Once the school stoops to meet the student, the standards of judgment begin to topple at all levels. As standards are lowered—as they cease to be the measure of the students and come to be measured by them—it becomes manifestly less possible for students to fail. But for the same reason it becomes less possible for them to learn and for teachers to teach.

The question, then, is what is to determine the pattern of education. Shall we shape a university education according to the previous schooling of the students, which we suppose has made them unfit to meet high expectations and standards, and to the supposed needs of students in some future still dark to us all? Or shall we shape it according to the nature and demands of the "leading Precognita of all things"—that is, according to the essential subjects of study? If we shape education to fit the students, then we clearly can maintain no standards; we will lose the subjects and eventually will lose the students as well. If we shape it to the subjects, then we will save both the subjects and the students. The inescapable purpose of education must be to preserve and pass on the essential human means—the thoughts and words and works and ways and standards and hopes without which we are not human. To preserve these things and to pass them on is to prepare students for life.

That such work cannot be done without high standards ought not to have to be said. There are necessarily increasing degrees of complexity in the studies as students rise through the grades and the years, and yet the standards remain the same. The first-graders, that is, must read and write in simple sentences, but they read and write, even so, in the language of the King James Bible, of Shakespeare and Johnson, of Thoreau, Whitman, Dickinson, and Twain. The grade-schooler and the graduate student must study the same American history, and there is no excuse for falsifying it in order to make it elementary.

Moreover, if standards are to be upheld, they cannot be specialized, professionalized, or departmented. Only common standards can be upheld—standards that are held and upheld in common by the whole community. When, in a university, for instance, English composition is made the responsibility exclusively of the English department, or of the subdepartment of freshman English, then the quality of the work in composition courses declines and the standards decline. This happens necessarily and for an obvious reason: If students' writing is graded according to form and quality in composition class but according only to "content" in, say, history class and if in other classes students are not required to write at all, then the message to the students is clear: namely, that the form and quality of their writing matters only in composition class, which is to say that it matters very little indeed. High standards of composition can be upheld only if they are upheld everywhere in the university.

Not only must the standards be held and upheld in common but they must also be applied fairly—that is, there must be no conditions with respect to persons or groups. There must be no discrimination for or against any person for any reason. The quality of the individual performer is the issue, not the category of the performer. The aim is to recognize, reward, and promote good work. Special pleading for "disadvantaged" groups— whether disadvantaged by history, economics, or education— can only make it increasingly difficult for members of that group to do good work and have it recognized.

If the university faculties have failed to answer the question of the internal placement of the knowledges of the arts and sciences with respect to each other and to the university as a whole, they have, it seems to me, also failed to ask the question of the external placement of these knowledges with respect to truth and to the world. This, of course, is a dangerous question, and I raise it with appropriate fear. The danger is that such questions should be *settled* by any institution whatever; these questions are the proper business of the people in the institutions, not of the institutions as such. I am arguing here against the specialist absorption in career and procedure that destroys what I take to be the indispensable interest in the question of the truth of what is taught and learned, as well as the equally indispensable interest in the fate and the use of knowledge in the world.

I would be frightened to hear that some university had suddenly taken a lively interest in the question of what is true and was in the process of answering it, perhaps by a faculty vote. But I am equally frightened by the fashionable lack of interest in the question among university teachers individually. I am more frightened when this disinterest, under the alias of "objectivity," is given the status of a public virtue.

Objectivity, in practice, means that one studies or teaches one's subject *as such,* without concern for its relation to other subjects or to the world—that is, without concern for its truth. If one is concerned, if one cares, about the truth or falsity of anything, one cannot be objective: one is glad if it is true and sorry if it is false; one believes it if it is judged to be true and disbelieves it if it is judged to be false. Moreover, the truth or falsity of some things cannot be objectively demonstrated, but must be determined by feeling and appearance, intuition and experience. And this work of judgment cannot take place at all with respect to one thing or one subject alone. The issue of truth rises out of the comparison of one thing with another, out of the study of the relations and influences between one thing and another and between one thing and many others.

Thus, if teachers aspire to the academic virtue of objectivity, they must teach as if their subject has nothing to do with anything beyond itself. The teacher of literature, for example, must propose the study of poems as relics left by people who, unlike our highly favored modern selves, believed in things not subject to measurable proof; religious poetry, that is, may be taught as having to do with matters once believed but not believable. The poetry is to be learned *about;* to learn *from* it would be an embarrassing betrayal of objectivity.

That this is more than a matter of classroom technique is made sufficiently evident in the current fracas over the teaching of the Bible in public schools. Judge Jackson Kiser of the federal district court in Bristol, Virginia, recently ruled that it would be constitutional to teach the Bible to public school students if the course is offered as an elective and "taught in an objective manner with no attempt made to indoctrinate the children as to either the truth or falsity of the biblical materials." James J. Kilpatrick, who discussed this ruling approvingly in one of his columns, suggested that the Bible might be taught "as Shakespeare is taught" and that this would be good because "the Bible is a rich lode of allusion, example and quotation." He warned that "The line that divides propaganda from instruction is a wavering line drawn on shifting sands," and he concluded by asserting that "Whatever else the Bible may be, the Bible is in fact literature. The trick is to teach it that way."[5]

The interesting question here is not whether young English-speakers should know the Bible—they obviously should—but whether a book that so directly offers itself to our belief or disbelief can be taught "as literature." It clearly cannot be so taught except by ignoring "whatever else [it] may be," which is a very substantial part of it. The question, then, is whether it can be adequately or usefully taught as something less than it is. The fact is that the writers of the Bible did not think that they were writing what Judge Kiser and Mr. Kilpatrick call "literature." They thought they were writing the truth, which they expected to be believed by some and disbelieved by others. It is conceivable that the Bible could be well taught by a teacher who believes that it is true, by a teacher who believes that it is untrue, or by a teacher who believes that it is partly true. That it could be well taught by a teacher uninterested in the question of its truth is not conceivable. That a lively interest in the Bible could be maintained through several generations of teachers uninterested in the question of its truth is also not conceivable.

Obviously, this issue of the Bible in the public schools cannot be resolved by federal court decisions that prescribe teaching methods. It can only be settled in terms of the freedom of teachers to teach as they believe and in terms of the relation of teachers and schools to their local communities. It may be that in this controversy we are seeing the breakdown of the public school system, as an inevitable consequence of the breakdown of local communities. It is hard to believe that this can be remedied in courts of law.

My point, anyhow, is that we could not consider teaching the Bible "as literature" if we were not already teaching literature "as literature"—as if we do not care, as if it does not matter, whether or not it is true. The causes of this are undoubtedly numerous, but prominent among them is a kind of shame among teachers of literature and other "humanities" that their truths are not objectively provable as are the truths of science. There is now an embarrassment about any statement that depends for confirmation upon experience or imagination or feeling or faith, and this embarrassment has produced an overwhelming impulse to treat such statements merely as artifacts, cultural relics, bits of historical evidence, or things of "aesthetic value." We will study, record, analyze, criticize, and appreciate. But we will not believe; we will not, in the full sense, know.

The result is a stance of "critical objectivity" that causes many teachers, historians, and critics of literature to sound—not like mathematicians or chemists: their methodology does not permit that yet—but like ethologists, students of the behavior of a species to which they do not belong, in whose history and fate they have no part, their aim being, not to know anything for themselves, but to "advance knowledge." This may be said to work, as a textual mechanics, but it is not an approach by which one may know any great work of literature. That route is simply closed to people interested in what "they" thought "then"; it is closed to people who think that "Dante's world" or "Shakespeare's world" is far removed and completely alienated from "our world"; and it is closed to the viewers of poetic devices, emotional effects, and esthetic values.

The great distraction behind the modern fate of literature, I think, is expressed in Coleridge's statement that his endeavor in *Lyrical Ballads* was "to transfer from our inward nature . . . a semblance of truth sufficient to procure for these shadows of imagination that willing suspension of disbelief for the moment, which constitutes poetic faith."[6] That is a sentence full of quakes and tremors. Is our inward nature true only by semblance? What is the difference, in a work of art, between truth and "semblance of truth"? What must be the result of separating "poetic faith" from faith of any other kind and then of making "poetic faith" dependent upon will?

The gist of the problem is in that adjective *willing*, which implies the superiority of the believer to what is believed. This implication, I am convinced, is simply untrue. Belief precedes will. One either believes or one does not, and, if one believes, then one willingly believes. If one disbelieves, even unwillingly, all the will in the world cannot make one believe. Belief is involuntary, as is the Ancient Mariner's recognition of the beauty and sanctity of the water snakes:

> A spring of love gushed from my heart,
> And I blessed them unaware . . .

This involuntary belief is the only approach to the great writings. One may, assuredly, not believe, and we must, of course, grant unbelievers the right to read and comment as unbelievers, for disbelief is a legitimate response, because it is a possible one. We must be aware of the possibility that belief may be false, and of the need to awaken from false belief; "one need not step into belief as into an abyss."[7] But we must be aware also that to disbelieve is to remain, in an important sense, outside the work. When we are *in* the work, we are long past the possibility of any debate with ourselves about whether or not to be willing to believe. When we are *in* the work, we simply *know* that great Odysseus has come home, that Dante is in the presence of the celestial rose, that Cordelia, though her father carries her in his arms, is dead. If we know these things, we are apt to know too that Mary Magdalene mistook the risen Christ for the gardener—and are thus eligible to be taken lightly by objective scholars, and to be corrected by a federal judge.

We and these works meet in imagination; by imagination we know their truth. In imagination, there is no specifically or exclusively "poetic faith," just as there is no faith that is specifically or exclusively religious. Belief is the same wherever it happens, and its terms are invariably set by the imagination. One believes, that is, because one *sees,* not because one is informed. That is why, four hundred years after Copernicus, we still say, "The sun is rising."

When we read the ballad of Sir Patrick Spens we know that the knight and his men have drowned because "Thair hats they swam aboone," not because we have confirmed the event by the study of historical documents. And if our assent is forced also by the ballad of Thomas Rhymer, far stranger than that of Sir Patrick, what are we to say? Must we go, believing, into the poem, and then return from it in disbelief because we find the story in no official record, have read of no such thing in the newspaper, and know nothing like it in our own experience? Or must we live with the poem, with our awareness of its power over us, as a piece of evidence that reality may be larger than we thought?

"Does that mean," I am asked, "that it's not possible for us to read Homer properly because we don't believe in the Greek gods?" I can only answer that I suspect that a proper reading of Homer will *result* in some manner of belief in his gods. How else explain their survival in the works of Christian writers into our own time? This survival has its apotheosis, it seems to me, in C. S. Lewis's novel, *That Hideous Strength,* at the end of which the Greek planetary deities reappear on earth as angels. Lewis wrote as a Christian who had read Homer, but he had read, obviously, as a man whose imagination was not encumbered with any such clinical apparatus as the willing suspension of disbelief. As such a reader, though he was a Christian, his reading had told him that the pagan gods retained a certain authority and commanded a certain assent. Like many of his forebears in English literary tradition, he yearned toward them. Their triumphant return, at the end of *That Hideous Strength,* as members of the heavenly hierarchy of Christianity, is not altogether a surprise. It is a profound resolution, not only in the novel itself, but in the history of English literature. One hears the ghosts of Spenser and Milton sighing with relief.

Questions of the authenticity of imaginings invite answers, and yet may remain unanswered. For the imagination is not always subject to immediate proof or demonstration. It is often subject only to the slow and partial authentication of experience. It is subject, that is, to a practical, though not an exact, validation, and it is subject to correction. For a work of imagination to endure through time, it must prove valid, and it must survive correction. It is correctable by experience, by critical judgment, and by further works of imagination.

To say that a work of imagination is subject to correction is, of course, to imply that there is no "world of imagination" as distinct from or opposed to the "real world." The imagination is *in* the world, is at work in it, is necessary to it, and is correctable by it. This correcting of imagination by experience is inescapable, necessary, and endless, as is the correcting of experience by imagination. This is the great general work of criticism to which we all are called. It is not literary criticism any more than it is historical or agricultural or biological criticism, but it must nevertheless be a fundamental part of the work of literary criticism, as it must be of criticisms of all other kinds. One of the most profound of human needs is for the truth of imagination to prove itself in every life and place in the world, and for the truth of the world's lives and places to be proved in imagination.

This need takes us as far as possible from the argument for works of imagination, human artifacts, as special cases, privileged somehow to offer themselves to the world on their own terms. It is this argument and the consequent abandonment of the general criticism that have permitted the universities to organize themselves on the industrial principle, as if faculties and students and all that they might teach and learn are no more than parts of a machine, the purpose of which they have, in general, not bothered to define, much less to question. And largely through the agency of the universities, this principle and this metaphor now dominate our relation to nature and to one another.

If, for the sake of its own health, a university must be interested in the question of the truth of what it teaches, then, for the sake of the world's health, it must be interested in the fate of that truth and the uses made of it in the world. It must want to know where its graduates live, where they work, and what they do. Do they return home with their knowledge to enhance and protect the life of their neighborhoods? Do they join the "upwardly mobile" professional force now exploiting and destroying local communities, both human and natural, all over the country? Has the work of the university, over the last generation, increased or decreased literacy and knowledge of the classics? Has it increased or decreased the general understanding of the sciences? Has it increased or decreased pollution and soil erosion? Has it increased or decreased the ability and the willingness of public servants to tell the truth? Such questions are not, of course, precisely answerable. Questions about influence never are. But they are askable, and the asking, should we choose to ask, would be a unifying and a shaping force.

NOTES

1. Eric Gill, *A Holy Tradition of Working,* ed. Brian Keeble (Ipswich: Golgonooza Press, 1983), p. 61.
2. W. Jackson Bate, *Samuel Johnson* (New York: Harcourt Brace Jovanovich, 1977), p. 51.
3. H. J. Massingham, *The Tree of Life* (London: Chapman & Hall, 1943).
4. "Texas School Board Chief Wants Sixth-Graders to Pick Job 'Tracks,'" *Courier-Journal* (Louisville, Ky.) 13 Aug. 1983.
5. "Plan to Teach the Bible as Literature May Wind up in the Supreme Court," *Courier-Journal* (Louisville, Ky.) 15 Sept. 1983.
6. Samuel Coleridge, *Biographia Literaria*, chapter 14.
7. Harry Mason, in a letter to the author.

Property, Patriotism, and National Defense

> Man cannot so far know the connexion of causes and events, as that he may venture to do wrong in order to do right. SAMUEL JOHNSON, *Rasselas*

> If it were a question of defending rivers, hills, mountains, skies, winds, rains, I would say, 'Willingly. That is our job. Let us fight. All our happiness in life is there.' No, we have defended the sham name of all that. JEAN GIONO, *Blue Boy*

1984

The present situation with regard to "national defense," as I believe that we citizens are now bidden to understand it, is that we, our country, and our governing principles of religion and politics are so threatened by a foreign enemy that we must prepare for a sacrifice that makes child's play of the "supreme sacrifices" of previous conflicts. We are asked, that is, not simply to "die in defense of our country," but to accept and condone the deaths of virtually the whole population of our country, of our political and religious principles, and of our land itself, as a reasonable cost of national defense.

That a nation should purchase at an exorbitant price and then rely upon a form of defense inescapably fatal to itself is, of course, absurd; that good citizenship should be defined as willing acceptance of such a form of defense can only be ruinous of the political health of that nation. To ask intelligent citizens to believe an argument that in its essentials is not arguable and to approve results that are not imaginably good (and in the strict sense are not imaginable at all) is to drive wedges of disbelief and dislike between those citizens and their government. Thus the effect of such a form of defense is ruinous, whether or not it is ever used.

The absurdity of the argument lies in a little-noted law of the nature of technology—that, past a certain power and scale, we do not dictate our terms to the tools we use; rather, the tools dictate their terms to us. Past a certain power and scale, we may choose the means but not the ends. We may choose nuclear weaponry as a form of defense, but that is the last of our "free choices" with regard to nuclear weaponry. By that choice we largely abandon ourselves to terms and results dictated by the nature of nuclear weapons. To take up weapons has, of course, always been a limiting choice, but never before has the choice been made by so few with such fatal implications for so many and so much. Once we have chosen to rely on such weapons, the only *free* choice we have left is to change our minds, to choose *not* to rely on them. "Good" or "humane" choices short of that choice involve a logic that is merely pitiful.

In order to attack our enemies with nuclear weapons, we must hate those enemies enough to kill them, and this hatred must be prepared in advance of any occasion or provocation. In order to work this hatred must be formalized in devices, systems, and procedures before any cause for the hatred exists.

And this hatred must be complete; there can be nothing selective about it. To use nuclear weapons against our enemies, we must hate them all enough to kill them. In this way, the technology dictates terms to its users. Our nuclear weapons articulate a perfect hatred, such as none of us has ever felt, or can feel, or can imagine feeling. In order to make a nuclear attack against the Russians, we must hate the innocent as well as the guilty, the children as well as the grown-ups. Thus, though it may be humanly impossible for us to propose it, we allow our technology to propose for us the defense of Christian love and justice (as we invariably put it) by an act of perfect hatred and perfect injustice. Or, as a prominent "conservative" columnist once put it, in order to save civilization we must become uncivilized.

The absurdity does not stop with the death of all of our enemies and all of our principles. It does not stop anywhere. Our nuclear weapons articulate for us a hatred of the Russian country itself: the land, water, air, light, plants, and animals of Russia. Those weapons will enact for us a perfect political hatred of birds and fish and trees. They will enact for us, too, a perfect hatred of ourselves, for a part of the inescapable meaning of those weapons is that we must hate our enemies so perfectly that in order to destroy them we are willing to destroy ourselves and everything dear that belongs to us.

The intention to use nuclear weapons appears to nullify every reason to use them, since there is no ostensible or imaginable reason for using them that could hope to survive their use. They would destroy all that they are meant to protect. There is no peace in them, or hope, or freedom, or health, or neighborliness, or justice, or love.

Except in the extremity of its immediate threat, nuclear weaponry is analogous to the inflated rhetoric of factional and political quarrels. It is too general and too extreme to be meant by any individual person; belief in the propriety of its use requires personal abandonment to a public passion not validated by personal experience. Nuclear behavior is thus like the behavior of the prejudices of race, class, or party: it issues a general condemnation for a cause that cannot prove sufficient.

As against political and factional rhetoric, the only defense against nuclear weaponry is dissent: the attempt to bring the particularizing intelligence to the real ground of the problem.

Since I am outlining here the ground of my own dissent, I should say that I am not by principle a passive man, or by nature a pacific one. I understand hatred and enmity very well from my own experience. Defense, moreover, is congenial to me, and I am willingly, sometimes joyfully, a defender of some things—among them, the principles and practices of democracy and Christianity that nuclear weapons are said to defend. I do not want to live under a government like that of Soviet Russia, and I would go to considerable trouble to avoid doing so.

I am not dissenting because I want the nation—that is, the country, its lives and its principles—to be undefended. I am dissenting because I no longer believe that the standing policy on national defense can defend the nation. And I am dissenting because the means employed, the threatened results, and the economic and moral costs have all become so extreme as to be unimaginable.

It is, to begin with, impossible for me to imagine that our "nuclear preparedness" is well understood or sincerely meant by its advocates in the government, much less by the nation at large. What we are proposing to ourselves and to the world is that we are prepared to die, to the last child, to the last green leaf, in defense of our dearest principles of liberty, charity, and justice. It would normally be expected, I think, that people led to the brink of total annihilation by so high and sober a purpose would be living lives of great austerity, sacrifice, and selfless discipline. That we are not doing so is a fact notorious even among ourselves. Our leaders are not doing so, nor are they calling upon us or preparing us to do so. As a people, we are selfish, greedy, dependent, and negligent of our duties to our land and to each other. We are evidently willing to sacrifice our own lives and the lives of millions of others, born and unborn—but not one minute of pleasure. We will have more arms, but not more taxes; we will aggrandize the military-industrial establishment, but not at the cost of self-aggrandizement. We will have defense and self-indulgence, which is to say, defense and debt. Surely not many nations before us have espoused bankruptcy and suicide as forms of self-defense.

This policy of national defense by national debt, so ruinous to the country as a whole, is exploited for profit and power by a subversive alliance of politicians, military officers, industrialists, and financiers—who, secure in their assumption that they will be the last to suffer or die as a result of their purposes, shift the real burden of industrial militarism onto the livelihoods of working people and onto the lives of young recruits.

Our alleged willingness to die for high principles, then, is all whitewash. We are not actually prepared to die for anything; we are merely resigned to the sham piety and the real greed of those in power.

What would make this willingness, this "state of nuclear preparedness," believable? It is easy enough to suggest some possible measures, both reasonable and necessary:

1. Forbid all taking of profit from military industries. Put an end to the possibility that anyone could get rich from any military enterprise. If all are asked to sacrifice their lives, why should not a few be asked to sacrifice their profits? If high principle is thought a sufficient motive for many, why should the profit motive be considered indispensable for a few?

2. Recognize that the outbreak of war in any form is a *failure* of government and of statesmanship. Let those who make or allow any war be the first into battle.

3. Require *all* the able-bodied to serve. Old and young alike have fought before in wars of national defense, such as the American Revolution, and they should be expected to do so again; "able-bodied" should mean "able to walk and to work." So far as possible, exemptions should be granted to the young, who have the greatest number of useful years still to live and have had the least time to understand the principles we wish to defend.

Let us assume, for the moment, that the argument of our present defense policy is valid, that our country, our lives, and our principles are indeed under threat of absolute destruction, and that our only possible defense against this threat is to hold the same absolute threat over our enemies—let us assume, in other words, that we have no choice but to accede to and pay for, the industry, the bureaucracy, and the politics of nuclear war. Let us assume that nuclear war is survivable and can be won and that the credibility of our will to wage such war might be established beyond suspicion. *Then* would those of us who care about the defense of our country, its lives, and its principles have anything to worry about?

We would still have a great deal to worry about, for we still would not have shown that the present version of national defense could really defend what we must mean when we speak of "the country, its lives, and its principles." We must ask if the present version of national defense is, in fact, national defense.

To answer that question, we must ask first what kind of country is defensible, militarily or in any other way. And we may answer that a defensible country has a large measure of practical and material independence: that it can live, if it has to, independent of foreign supplies and of long distance transport within its own boundaries. It must also rest upon the broadest possible base of economic prosperity, not just in the sense of a money economy, but in the sense of properties, materials, and practical skills. Most important of all, it must be generally loved and competently cared for by its people, who, individually, identify their own interest with the interest of their neighbors and of the country (the land) itself.

To a considerable extent, that is the kind of country we had from the Revolution through World War II—and, to an even more considerable extent, that is the kind of country a great many people *hoped* to have during that time—which largely explains why the country was then so well defended. The remains and relics of that country are still scattered about us. The ideal or the fact of local independence is still alive in some individuals, some communities, and some small localities. There remain, here and there, a declining number of small farms, shops, stores, and other small enterprises that suggest the possibility of a broad, democratic distribution of usable property. If one hunts for them, one can still find small parcels and plots of our land that have been cared for and safeguarded in use, not by the abstract political passion that now disgraces the name of patriotism, for such passion does not do such work, but by personal knowledge, affection, responsibility, and skill.

And even today, against overpowering odds and prohibitive costs, one does not have to go far in any part of the country to hear voiced the old hopes that stirred millions of immigrants, freed slaves, westward movers, young couples starting out: a little farm, a little shop, a little store—some kind of place and enterprise of one's own, within and by which one's family could achieve a proper measure of independence, not only of economy, but of satisfaction, thought, and character.

That our public institutions have not looked with favor upon these hopes is sufficiently evident from the results. In the first twenty-five years after World War II, our farm people were driven off their farms by economic pressure at the rate of about one million a year. They are still going out of business at the rate of 1,400 farm families per week, or 72,800 families per year. That the rate of decline is now less than it was does not mean that the situation is improving; it means that the removal of farmers from farming is nearly complete. Less than 3 percent of the population of our country is left on the farms; that tiny percentage is presently declining and, if present conditions continue, will certainly decline further. Of that tiny percentage, a percentage still tinier now owns most of the land and produces most of the food. *Farming,* the magazine of the Production Credit Association, told farmers in its issue for March/April 1984: "Projections are that within the next 10 to 15 years, there'll be 200,000 to 300,000 of you farming big enough to account for 90% of the nation's gross farm receipts."

But this is not happening just on the farm. A similar decline is taking place in the cities. According to Joel Havemann, in the *Los Angeles Times,* 10 December, 1983, "The percentage of households that own their own homes fell from 65.6 percent in 1980 to 64.5 at the end of 1982." Those percentages are too low in a country devoted to the defense of private ownership, and the decline is ominous. The reasons were the familiar ones of inflation and usury: "During the 1970's, the value of a median-priced home nearly tripled, while family income only doubled and mortgage interest rates rocketed to a peak of more than 16 percent in late 1981." And in The *Atlantic Monthly* of September 1984, Philip Langdon wrote: "Most families are priced out of the new-home market and have been for years. In April the median price of a new single-family house rose above $80,000—an increase of 24 percent since 1979 . . ."

Those of us who can remember as far back as World War II do not need statistics to tell us that in the last forty years the once plentiful small, privately owned neighborhood groceries, pharmacies, restaurants, and other small shops and businesses have become endangered species, in many places extinct. It is this as much as anything that has rotted the hearts of our cities and surrounded them with shopping centers built by the corporate competitors of the small owners. The reasons, again, are inflation and usury, as well as the legally sanctioned advantages of corporations in their competition with individuals. Since World War II, the money interest has triumphed over the property interest, to the inevitable decline of the good care and the good use of property.

As a person living in a rural, agricultural community, I need no statistics to inform me of the decline in the availability of essential goods and services in such places. Welders, carpenters, masons, mechanics, electricians, plumbers—all are in short supply, and their decline in the last ten years has been precipitous. Because of high interest rates and inflation, properties, tools, and supplies have become so expensive as to put a small business out of reach of many who would otherwise be willing. High interest works directly to keep local capital from being put to work locally.

When inflation and interest rates are high, young people starting out in small businesses or on small farms must pay a good living every year for the privilege of earning a poor one. People who are working are paying an exorbitant tribute to people who are, as they say, "letting their money work for them." The abstract value of money is preying upon and destroying the particular values that inhere in the lives of the land and of its human communities. For many years now, our officials have been bragging about the immensity of our gross national product and of the growth of our national economy, apparently without recognizing the possibility that the national economy as a whole can grow (up to a point) by depleting or destroying the small local economies within it.

The displacement of millions of people over the last forty or fifty years has, of course, been costly. The costs are not much talked about by apologists for our economy, and they have not been deducted from national or corporate incomes, but the costs exist nevertheless and they are not to be dismissed as intangible; to a considerable extent they have to do with the destruction and degradation of property. The decay of the inner parts of our cities is one of the costs; another is soil erosion, and other forms of land loss and land destruction; another is pollution.

There seems to be no escape from the requirement that intensive human *use* of property, if it is not to destroy the property, must be accompanied by intensive—that is, intimate—human care. It is often assumed that ownership guarantees good care, but that is not necessarily true. It has long been understood that absentee ownership is a curse upon property. Corporate ownership is plagued by the incompetence, irresponsibility, or antipathy of employees. And among us, at least, public ownership, as of waterways and roads, amounts virtually to an invitation to abuse. Good use of property, then, seems to require not only ownership but personal occupation and use by the owner. That is to say that the good use of property requires the widest possible distribution of ownership.

When urban property is gathered into too few hands and when the division between owners and users becomes therefore too great, a sort of vengeance is exacted upon urban property:

people litter their streets and destroy their dwellings. When rural property is gathered into too few hands, even when, as in farming, the owners may still be the users, there is an inevitable shift of emphasis from maintenance to production, and the land deteriorates. People displaced from farming have been replaced by machines, chemicals, and other technological "labor-savers" that, of themselves, contribute to production, but do not, of themselves, contribute to maintenance, and often, of themselves, contribute to the degradation both of the land and of human care for it. Thus, our extremely serious problems of soil erosion and of pollution by agricultural chemicals are both attributable to the displacement of people from agriculture. The technologies of "agribusiness" are enabling less than 3 percent of our people to keep the land in production (for the time being), but they do not and cannot enable them to take care of it.

Increasing the number of property owners is not in itself, of course, a guarantee of better use. People who do not know how to care for property cannot care for it, no matter how willing they may be to do so. But good care is potential in the presence of people, no matter how ignorant; there is no hope of it at all in their absence. The question bearing ever more heavily upon us is how this potential for good care in people may be developed and put to use. The honest answer, at present, seems to be that we do not know how. Perhaps we will have to begin by answering the question negatively. For example, most people who move from place to place every few years will never learn to care well for any place, nor will most people who are long alienated from all responsibility for usable property. Such people, moreover, cannot be taught good care by books or classroom instruction, nor can it be forced upon them by law. A people as a whole can learn good care only by long experience of living and working, learning and remembering, in the same places generation after generation, experiencing and correcting the results of bad care, and enjoying the benefits of good care.

It may be, also, that people who do not care well *for* their land will not care enough *about* it to defend it well. It seems certain that people who hope to be capable of national defense in the true sense—not by invading foreign lands but by driving off invaders of their own land—must love their country with the particularizing passion with which settled people have always loved, not their nation, but their *homes,* their daily lives and daily bread.

An abstract nationalist patriotism may be easy to arouse, if the times offer a leader sufficiently gifted in the manipulation of crowds, but it is hard to sustain, and it has the seed of a foolishness in it that will become its disease. Our great danger at present is that we have no defensive alternative to this sort of hollow patriotic passion and its inevitable expression in nuclear warheads; this is both because our people are too "mobile" to have developed strong local loyalties and strong local economies and because the nation is thus made everywhere locally vulnerable—indefensible except as a whole. Our life no longer rests broadly upon our land but has become an inverted pyramid resting upon the pinpoint of a tiny, dwindling, agricultural minority critically dependent upon manufactured supplies and upon credit. Moreover, the population as a whole is now dependent upon goods and services that are not and often cannot be produced locally but must be transported, often across the entire width of the continent or from the other side of the world. Our national livelihood is everywhere pinched into wires, pipelines, and roads. A fact that cannot have eluded our military experts is that this "strongest nation in the world" is almost pitifully vulnerable on its own ground. A relatively few well-directed rifle shots, a relatively few well-placed sticks of dynamite could bring us to darkness, confusion, and hunger. And this civil weakness serves and aggravates the military obsession with megatonnage. It is only logical that a nation weak at home should threaten abroad with whatever destructions its technology can contrive. It is logical, but it is mad.

Nor can it have eluded our military experts that our own Revolution was won, in spite of the gravest military disadvantages, by a farmer-soldiery, direct shareholders in their country, who were therefore, as Jefferson wrote, "wedded to its liberty and its interests, by the most lasting bonds." The Persian Wars, according to Aubrey de Sélincourt, "proved to the Greeks what a handful of free men, fighting for what they loved, could achieve against a horde of invaders advancing to battle 'under the lash . . .'" And though the circumstances are inevitably different, we should probably draw similar conclusions from our experience in Vietnam, and from the Soviet Union's in Afghanistan. People tend to fight well in defense of their homes—the prerequisite being, of course, that they must have homes to defend. That is, they must not look on their dwelling places as dispensable or disposable campsites on the way to supposedly better dwelling places. A highly mobile population is predisposed to retreat; its values propose no sufficient reason for anyone to stay anywhere. The hope of a defensive *stand* had better rest on settled communities, whose ways imply their desire to be permanent.

I have been arguing from what seems to me a reasonable military assumption: that a sound policy of national defense would have its essential foundation and its indispensable motives in widespread, settled, thriving local communities, each having a proper degree of independence, living so far as possible from local sources, and using its local sources with a stewardly care that would sustain its life indefinitely, even through times of adversity. But now I would like to go further, and say that such communities, where they exist, are not merely the prerequisites or supports of a sound national defense; they *are* a sound national defense. They defend the country daily and hourly in all their acts by taking care of it, by causing it to thrive, by giving it the health and the satisfactions that make it worth defending, and by teaching these things to the young. This, to my mind, is *real* national defense, and military national defense would come from it, as if by nature, when occasion demanded, as the history of our Revolution suggests. To neglect such national defense, to destroy the possibility of it, in favor of a highly specialized, expensive, unwieldy, inflexible, desperate, and suicidal reliance on nuclear weapons is already to be defeated.

It is not as though the two kinds of national defense are compatible; it is not as though settled, stewardly communities can thrive and at the same time support a nuclear arsenal. In fact, the present version of national defense is destroying its own supports in the land and in human communities, for not only does it foster apathy, cynicism, and despair, especially in the young, but it is directly destructive of land and people by the inflation and usury that it encourages. The present version of national defense, like the present version of agriculture, rests upon debt—a debt that is driving up the cost of interest and driving down the worth of money, putting the national government actively in competition against good young people who are striving to own their own small farms and small businesses.

People who are concerned with the work of what I have called real national defense will necessarily have observed that it must be carried out often against our national government, and unremittingly against our present national economy. And our political and military leaders should have noticed, if they have not, that, whereas most of the citizenry now submit apathetically or cynically to the demands and costs of so-called national defense, works and acts of real national defense are being carried out locally in all parts of the country every day with firm resolve and with increasing skill. People, local citizens, are getting together, without asking for or needing governmental sanction, to defend their rivers, hills, mountains, skies, winds, and rains. They are doing this ably, peaceably, and many times successfully, though they are still far from the success that they desire.

The costs of this state of affairs to our instituted government are many and dangerous; perhaps they may best be suggested by questions. To what point, for instance, do we defend from foreign enemies a country that we are destroying ourselves? In spite of all our propagandists can do, the foreign threat inevitably seems diminished when our air is unsafe to breathe, when our drinking water is unsafe to drink, when our rivers carry tonnages of topsoil that make light of the freight they carry in boats, when our forests are dying from air pollution and acid rain, and when we ourselves are sick from poisons in the air. Who *are* the enemies of this country? This is a question dangerous to instituted government when people begin to ask it for themselves. Many who have seen forests clear-cut on steep slopes, who have observed the work of the strip miners, who have watched as corporations advance their claims on private property "in the public interest," are asking that question already. Many more are going to ask.

Millions of people, moreover, who have lost small stores, shops, and farms to corporations, money merchants, and usurers, will continue to be asked to defend capitalism against communism. Sooner or later, they are going to demand to know why. If one must spend one's life as an employee, what difference does it make whether one's employer is a government or a corporation?

People, as history shows, will fight willingly and well to defend what they perceive as their own. But how willingly and how well will they fight to defend what has already been taken from them?

Finally, we must ask if international fighting as we have known it has not become obsolete in the presence of such omnivorous weapons as we now possess. There will undoubtedly always be a need to resist aggression, but now, surely, we must think of changing the means of such resistance.

In the face of all-annihilating weapons, the natural next step may be the use of no weapons. It may be that the only possibly effective defense against the ultimate weapon is no weapon at all. It may be that the presence of nuclear weapons in the world serves notice that the command to love one another is an absolute practical necessity, such as we never dreamed it to be before, and that our choice is not to win or lose, but to love our enemies or die.

Men and Women in Search of Common Ground

The domestic joys, the daily housework or business,
the building of houses—they are not phan-
tasms . . . they have weight and form and location . . .   WALT WHITMAN, *To Think of Time*

1985

I am not an authority on men or women or any of the possible
connections between them. In sexual matters I am an amateur, in
both the ordinary and the literal senses of that word. I speak
about them only because I am concerned about them; I am concerned about them only because I am involved in them; I am
involved in them, apparently, only because I am a human, a
qualification for which I deserve no credit.

I do not believe, moreover, that any individual *can* be an authority on the present subject. The common ground between
men and women can only be defined by community authority.
Individually, we may desire it and think about it, but we are not
going to occupy it if we do not arrive there together.

That we have not arrived there, that we apparently are not very
near to doing so, is acknowledged by the title of this symposium
["Men and Women in Search of Common Ground," a symposium at the Jung Institute of San Francisco]. And that a symposium so entitled should be held acknowledges implicitly that
we are not happy in our exile. The specific cause of our unhappi-
ness, I assume, is that relationships between men and women are

now too often extremely tentative and temporary, whereas we would like them to be sound and permanent.

Apparently, it is in the nature of all human relationships to aspire to be permanent. To propose temporariness as a goal in such relationships is to bring them under the rule of aims and standards that prevent them from beginning. Neither marriage, nor kinship, nor friendship, nor neighborhood can exist with a life expectancy that is merely convenient.

To see that such connections aspire to permanence, we do not have to look farther than popular songs, in which people still speak of loving each other "forever." We now understand, of course, that in this circumstance the word "forever" is not to be trusted. It may mean only "for a few years" or "for a while" or even "until tomorrow morning." And we should not be surprised to realize that if the word "forever" cannot be trusted in this circumstance, then the word "love" cannot be trusted either.

This, as we know, was often true before our own time, though in our time it seems easier than before to say "I will love you forever" and to mean nothing by it. It is possible for such words to be used cynically—that is, they may be *intended* to mean nothing—but I doubt that they are often used with such simple hypocrisy. People continue to use them, I think, because they continue to try to mean them. They continue to express their sexual feelings with words such as "love" and "forever" because they want those feelings to have a transferable value, like good words or good money. They cannot bear for sex to be "just sex," any more than they can bear for family life to be just reproduction or for friendship to be just a mutually convenient exchange of goods and services.

The questions that I want to address here, then, are: Why are sexual and other human relationships now so impermanent? And under what conditions might they become permanent?

It cannot be without significance that this division is occurring at a time when division has become our characteristic mode of thinking and acting. Everywhere we look now, the axework of division is going on. We see ourselves more and more as divided from each other, from nature, and from what our traditions define as human nature. The world is now full of nations, races, interests, groups, and movements of all sorts, most of them unable to define their relations to each other except in terms of division and opposition. The poor human body itself has been conceptually hacked to pieces and parceled out like a bureaucracy. Brain and brawn, left brain and right brain, stomach, hands, heart, and genitals have all been set up in competition against each other, each supported by its standing army of advocates, press agents, and merchants. In such a time, it is not surprising that the stresses that naturally, and perhaps desirably, occur between the sexes should result in the same sort of division with the same sort of doctrinal justification.

This condition of division is one that we suffer from and complain about, yet it is a condition that we promote by our ambitions and desires and justify by our jargon of "self-fulfillment." Each of us, we say, is supposed to "realize his or her full potential as an individual." It is as if the whole two hundred million of us were saying with Coriolanus:

> I'll never
> Be such a gosling to obey instinct, but stand
> As if a man were author of himself
> And knew no other kin.   (V, iii, 34–37)

By "instinct" he means the love of family, community, and country. In Shakespeare's time, this "instinct" was understood to be the human norm—the definition of humanity, or a large part of that definition. When Coriolanus speaks these lines, he identifies himself, not as "odd," but as monstrous, a *danger* to family, community, and country. He identifies himself, that is, as an individual prepared to act alone and without the restraint of reverence, fidelity, or love. Shakespeare is at one with his tradition in understanding that such a person acted inevitably, not as the "author of himself," but as the author of tragic consequences both for himself and for other people.

The problem, of course, is that we are *not* the authors of ourselves. That we are not is a religious perception, but it is also a biological and a social one. Each of us has had many authors, and each of us is engaged, for better or worse, in that same authorship. We could say that the human race is a great coauthorship in which we are collaborating with God and nature in the making of ourselves and one another. From this there is no escape. We may collaborate either well or poorly, or we may refuse to collaborate, but even to refuse to collaborate is to exert an influence and to affect the quality of the product. This is only a way of saying that by ourselves we have no meaning and no dignity; by ourselves we are outside the human definition, outside our identity. "More and more," Mary Catharine Bateson wrote in *With a Daughter's Eye*, "it has seemed to me that the idea of an individual, the idea that there is someone to be known, separate from the relationships, is simply an error."

Some time ago I was with Wes Jackson, wandering among the experimental plots at his home and workplace, the Land Institute in Salina, Kansas. We stopped by one plot that had been planted in various densities of population. Wes pointed to a Maximilian sunflower growing alone, apart from the others, and said, "There is a plant that has 'realized its full potential as an individual.'" And clearly it had: It had grown very tall; it had put out many long branches heavily laden with blossoms—and the branches had broken off, for they had grown too long and too heavy. The plant had indeed realized its full potential as an individual, but it had failed as a Maximilian sunflower. We could say that its full potential as an individual *was* this failure. It had failed because it had lived outside an important part of its definition, which consists of *both* its individuality and its community. A part of its properly realizable potential lay in its community, not in itself.

In making a metaphor of this sunflower, I do not mean to deny the value or the virtue of a *proper* degree of independence in the character and economy of an individual, nor do I mean to deny the conflicts that occur between individuals and communities. Those conflicts belong to our definition, too, and are probably as necessary as they are troublesome. I do mean to say that the conflicts are not everything, and that to make conflict—the so-called "jungle law"—the basis of social or economic doctrine is extremely dangerous. A part of our definition is our common ground, and a part of it is sharing and mutually enjoying our common ground. Undoubtedly, also, since we are humans, a part of our definition is a recurring contest over the common ground: Who shall describe its boundaries, occupy it, use it, or own it? But such contests obviously can be carried too far, so that they become destructive both of the commonality of the common ground and of the ground itself.

The danger of the phrase "common ground" is that it is likely to be meant as no more than a metaphor. I am *not* using it as a metaphor; I mean by it the actual ground that is shared by whatever group we may be talking about—the human race, a nation, a community, or a household. If we use the term only as a metaphor, then our thinking will not be robustly circumstantial and historical, as it needs to be, but only a weak, clear broth of ideas and feelings.

Marriage, for example, is talked about most of the time as if it were only a "human relationship" between a wife and a husband. A good marriage is likely to be explained as the result of mutually satisfactory adjustments of thoughts and feelings—a "deep" and complicated mental condition. That is surely true for some couples some of the time, but, as a general understanding of marriage, it is inadequate and probably unworkable. It is far too much a thing of the mind and, for that reason, is not to be trusted. "God guard me," Yeats wrote, "from those thoughts men think / In the mind alone . . ."

Yeats, who took seriously the principle of incarnation, elaborated this idea in his essay on the Japanese Noh plays, in which he says that "we only believe in those thoughts which have been conceived not in the brain but in the whole body." But we need a broader concept yet, for a marriage involves more than just the bodies and minds of a man and a woman. It involves locality, human circumstance, and duration. There is a strong possibility that the basic human sexual unit is composed of a man and a woman (bodies and minds), plus their history together, plus their kin and descendants, plus their place in the world with its economy and history, plus their natural neighborhood, plus their human community with its memories, satisfactions, expectations, and hopes.

By describing it in such a way, we begin to understand marriage as the insistently practical union that it is. We begin to understand it, that is, as it is represented in the traditional marriage ceremony, those vows being only a more circumstantial and practical way of saying what the popular songs say dreamily and easily: "I will love you forever"—a statement that, in this world, inescapably leads to practical requirements and consequences because it proposes survival as a goal. Indeed, marriage is a union much more than practical, for it looks both to our survival as a species and to the survival of our definition as human beings—that is, as creatures who make promises and keep them, who care devotedly and faithfully for one another, who care properly for the gifts of life in this world.

The business of humanity is undoubtedly survival in this complex sense—a necessary, difficult, and entirely fascinating job of work. We have in us deeply planted instructions—personal, cultural, and natural—to survive, and we do not need much experience to inform us that we cannot survive alone. The smallest possible "survival unit," indeed, appears to be the universe. At any rate, the ability of an organism to survive outside the universe has yet to be demonstrated. Inside it, everything happens *in concert*; not a breath is drawn but by the grace of an inconceivable series of vital connections joining an inconceivable multiplicity of created things in an inconceivable unity. But of course it is preposterous for a mere individual human to espouse the universe—a possibility that is purely mental, and productive of nothing but talk. On the other hand, it may be that our marriages, kinships, friendships, neighborhoods, and all our forms and acts of homemaking are the rites by which we solemnize and enact our union with the universe. These ways are practical, proper, available to everybody, and they can provide for the safekeeping of the small acreages of the universe that have been entrusted to us. Moreover, they give the word "love" its only chance to mean, for only they can give it a history, a community, and a place. Only in such ways can love become flesh and do its worldly work. For example, a marriage without a place, a household, has nothing to show for itself. Without a history of some length, it does not know what it means. Without a community to exert a shaping pressure around it, it may explode because of the pressure inside it.

These ways of marriage, kinship, friendship, and neighborhood surround us with forbiddings; they are forms of bondage, and involved in our humanity is always the wish to escape. We may be obliged to look on this wish as necessary, for, as I have just implied, these unions are partly shaped by internal pressure. But involved in our humanity also is the warning that we can escape only into loneliness and meaninglessness. Our choice may be between a small, human-sized meaning and a vast meaninglessness, or between the freedom of our virtues and the freedom of our vices. It is only in these bonds that our individuality has a use and a worth; it is only to the people who know us, love us, and depend on us that we are indispensable as the persons we uniquely are. In our industrial society, in which people insist so fervently on their value and their freedom "as individuals," individuals are seen more and more as "units" by their governments, employers, and suppliers. They live, that is, under the rule of the interchangeability of parts: What one person can do, another person can do just as well or a newer person can do better. Separate from the relationships, there is nobody to be known; people become, as they say and feel, nobodies.

It is plain that, under the rule of the industrial economy, humans, at least as individuals, are well advanced in a kind of obsolescence. Among those who have achieved even a modest success according to the industrial formula, the human body has been almost entirely replaced by machines and by a shrinking population of manual laborers. For enormous numbers of people now, the only physical activity that they cannot delegate to machines or menials, who will presumably do it more to their satisfaction, is sexual activity. For many, the only necessary physical labor is that of childbirth.

According to the industrial formula, the ideal human residence (from the Latin *residere,* "to sit back" or "remain sitting") is one in which the residers do not work. The house is built, equipped, decorated, and provisioned by other people, by strangers. In it, the married couple practice as few as possible of the disciplines of household or homestead. Their domestic labor consists principally of buying things, putting things away, and throwing things away, but it is understood that it is "best" to have even those jobs done by an "inferior" person, and the ultimate industrial ideal is a "home" in which *everything* would be done by pushing buttons. In such a "home," a married couple are mates, sexually, legally, and socially, but they are not helpmates; they do nothing useful either together or for each other. According to the ideal, work should be done *away* from home. When such spouses say to each other, "I will love you forever," the meaning of their words is seriously impaired by their circumstances; they are speaking in the presence of so little that they have done and made. Their history together is essentially placeless; it has no visible or tangible incarnation. They have only themselves in view.

In such a circumstance, the obsolescence of the body is inevitable, and this is implicitly acknowledged by the existence of the "physical fitness movement." Back in the era of the body, when women and men were physically useful as well as physically attractive to one another, physical fitness was simply a condition. Little conscious attention was given to it; it was a by-product of useful work. Now an obsessive attention has been fixed upon it. Physical fitness has become extremely mental; once free, it has become expensive, an industry—just as sexual attractiveness, once the result of physical vigor and useful work, has now become an industry. The history of "sexual liberation" has been a history of increasing bondage to corporations.

Now the human mind appears to be following the human body into obsolescence. Increasingly, jobs that once were done by the minds of individual humans are done by computers—and by governments and experts. Dr. William C. DeVries, the current superstar of industrial heart replacement, can blithely assure a reporter that "the general society is not very well informed to make those decisions [as to the imposition of restraints on medical experiments on human patients], and that's why the medical society or the government who has a wider range of view comes in to make those decisions" (Louisville *Courier-Journal*, 3 Feb. 1985). Thus we may benefit from the "miracles" of modern medical science on the condition that we delegate all moral and critical authority in such matters to the doctors and the government. We may save our bodies by losing our minds, just as, according to another set of experts, we may save our minds by forsaking our bodies. Computer thought is exactly the sort that Yeats warned us against; it is made possible by the assumption that thought occurs "in the mind alone" and that the mind, therefore, is an excerptable and isolatable human function, which can be set aside from all else that is human, reduced to pure process, and so imitated by a machine. But in fact we know that the *human* mind is not distinguishable from what it knows and that what it knows comes from or is radically conditioned by its embodied life in this world. A machine, therefore, cannot be a mind or be like a mind; it can only *replace* a mind.

We know, too, that these mechanical substitutions are part of a long-established process. The industrial economy has made its way among us by a process of division, degradation, and then replacement. It is only after we have been divided against each other that work and the products of work can be degraded; it is only after work and its products have been degraded that workers can be replaced by machines. Only when thought has been degraded can a mind be replaced by a machine, or a society of experts, or a government.

It is true, furthermore, that, in this process of industrialization, what is free is invariably replaced by a substitute that is costly. Bodily health as the result of useful work, for instance, is or was free, whereas industrial medicine, which has flourished upon the uselessness of the body, is damagingly and heartlessly expensive. In the time of the usefulness of the body, when the body became useless it died, and death was understood as a kind of healing; industrial medicine looks upon death as a disease that calls for increasingly expensive cures.

Similarly, in preindustrial country towns and city neighborhoods, the people who needed each other lived close to each other. This proximity was free, and it provided many benefits that were either free or comparatively cheap. This simple proximity has been destroyed and replaced by communications and transportation industries that are, again, enormously expensive and destructive, as well as extremely vulnerable to disruption.

Insofar as we reside in the industrial economy, our obsolescence, both as individuals and as humankind, is fast growing upon us. But we cannot regret or, indeed, even know that this is true without knowing and naming those never-to-be-official institutions that alone have the power to reestablish us in our true estate and identity: marriage, family, household, friendship, neighborhood, community. For these to have an effective existence, they must be located in the world and in time. So located, they have the power to establish us in our human identity because they are not merely institutions in a public, abstract sense, like the organized institutions but are also private conditions. They are the conditions in which a human is complete, body and mind, because completely necessary and needed.

When we live within these human enclosures, we escape the tyrannical doctrine of the interchangeability of parts; in these enclosures, we live as members, each in its own identity necessary to the others. When our spouse or child, friend or neighbor is in need or in trouble, we do not deal with them by means of a computer, for we know that, with them, we must not think without feeling. We do not help them by sending a machine, for we know that, with them, a machine cannot represent us. We know that, when they need us, we must go and offer ourselves, body and mind, as we are. As members, moreover, we are useless and worse than useless to each other if we do not care properly for the ground that is common to us.

It is only in these trying circumstances that human love is given its chance to have meaning, for it is only in these circumstances that it can be borne out in deeds through time—"even," to quote Shakespeare again, "to the edge of doom"—and thus prove itself true by fulfilling its true term.

In these circumstances, in place and in time, the sexes will find their common ground and be somewhat harmoniously rejoined, not by some resolution of conflict and power, but by proving indispensable to one another, as in fact they are.

Six Agricultural Fallacies

1985

1. *That agriculture may be understood and dealt with as an industry.*

This assumption is false, first of all, because agriculture deals with living things and biological processes, whereas the materials of industry are not alive and the processes are mechanical. That agriculture can produce only out of the lives of living creatures means that it cannot for very long escape the qualitative standard; that is, in addition to productivity, efficiency, decent earnings, and so on, it must have health. Thus, the farmer differs from the industrialist in that the farmer is necessarily a nurturer, a preserver of the health of creatures.

Second, whereas a factory has a limited life expectancy, the life of a healthy farm is unlimited. Buildings and tools wear out, but the topsoil, if properly used and maintained, will not wear out. Some agricultural soils have remained in continuous use for four or five thousand years or more.

Third, the motives of agriculture are fundamentally different from the motives of industry. This is partly accounted for by the differences between farming and industry that I have already mentioned. Another reason lies in the fact that, in our country and in many others, the best farms have always been homes as well as workplaces. Unlike factory hands and company executives, farmers do not *go* to work; a good farmer is *at* work even when at rest. Over and over again, experience has shown that the motives of the wage earner are inadequate to farming. American experience has shown this, but it is perhaps nowhere so dramatically demonstrated as in the Soviet Union, where small, privately farmed plots greatly outproduce the communal fields.

Finally, the economy of industry is inimical to the economy of agriculture. The economy of industry is, typically, an extractive economy: It takes, makes, uses, and discards; it progresses, that is, from exhaustion to pollution. Agriculture, on the other hand, rightly belongs to a replenishing economy, which takes, makes, uses, and *returns*. It involves the return to the source, not just of fertility or of so-called wastes, but also of care and affection. Otherwise, the topsoil is used exactly as a minable fuel and is destroyed in use. Thus, in agriculture, the methods of the factory give us the life expectancy of the factory—long enough for us, perhaps, but not long enough for our children and grandchildren.

2. *That a sound agricultural economy can be based on an export market.*

We should begin, I think, by assuming that a sound economy cannot be based on *any* market that it does not control.

We should assume, further, that any foreign market for food ought to be temporary and, therefore, by definition, not dependable. The best thing for any nation or people, obviously, is to grow its own food, and therefore charity alone would forbid us to depend on or to wish for a permanent market for our agricultural products in any foreign country. And we must ask, too, whether or not charity can ever regard hungry people as a "market."

But the commercial principle itself is unsafe in agriculture if it is not made subject to other principles, such as that of subsistence. Commercial farming must never be separated from subsistence farming; the farm family should live from the farm. Just as the farm should be, as much as possible, the source of its own fertility and operating energy, so it should be, as much as possible, the source of food, shelter, fuel, building materials, and so on for the farm family. In this way, the basic livelihood of the farming population is assured. In times such as these, when costs of purchased supplies are high and earnings from farm produce low, the value of whatever the farm family produces for itself is high and involves substantial savings. What is exported from the farm in whatever quantity, is properly regarded as surplus—what is not needed for subsistence.

At every level of the agricultural system, the subsistence principle should operate. The local consumer population in towns and cities should subsist, as much as possible, from the produce of the locality or region. The primary reason for this, in the region as on the farm, is that it is safe, but there are many other benefits: It would tend to diversify local farming as well as support the local farm economy. It would greatly reduce transportation and other costs, put fresher food on the table, and increase local employment. What would be exported from the region would, again, be regarded as surplus.

The same principle should then apply to the nation as a whole. We should subsist from our own land, and then the surplus would be available for export markets or for charity in emergencies.

The surplus should not be regarded as merely incidental to subsistence but as equally necessary for safety—a sort of "floating" supply usable to compensate for both differences and vagaries of climate. Because of drouths, floods, and storms, no farm, region, or even nation can be assured forever of a subsistence, and it is only because of this that an exportable surplus has a legitimate place in agricultural planning.

3. *That the "free market" can preserve agriculture.*
The "free market"—the unbridled play of economic forces—is bad for agriculture because it is unable to assign a value to

things that are necessary to agriculture. It gives a value to agricultural products, but it cannot give a value to the sources of those products in the topsoil, the ecosystem, the farm, the farm family, or the farm community. Indeed, people who look at farming from the standpoint of the "free market" do not understand the relation of product to source. They believe that the relation is merely mechanical because they believe that agriculture is or can be an industry. And the "free market" is helpless to suggest otherwise.

The "free market" values production *at the cost* of all else, and this exclusive emphasis on production, in agriculture, inevitably causes overproduction. In agriculture, both high prices and low prices cause overproduction, yet overproduction leads only to low prices, never to high prices. It could perhaps be said, then, that on the "free market" agricultural productivity has no direct or stable relation to value. When this is so, agriculture overproduces, and the surplus is used as a weapon against the producer to beat down prices, either in the service of a "cheap food policy" for domestic consumers or to make our agricultural produce competitive in world trade.

In a time when urban investment in agriculture (that is, "agribusiness") stimulates a higher productivity than the urban economy can provide a market for, then the rural economy can be protected only by controlling production. Supplies should be adjusted to anticipated needs, and those needs should always include surpluses to be used in case of crop failure. Such an adjustment can be only approximate, of course, but since we are dealing with an annual productivity, yearly corrections can be made. Thus, the sources of production can be preserved by preventing runaway surpluses and the consequent low markets that destroy both people and land.

The "free market" is economic Darwinism, with one critical qualification. Whereas the Darwinian biologists have always acknowledged the violence of the competitive principle, the political Darwinians have been unable to resist the temptation to suggest that on the "free market" *both* predator and prey are beneficiaries. When economic ruin occurs, according to this view, it occurs only as a result of economic justice. Thus, David Stockman could suggest that the present dispossession of thousands of farm families is merely the result of the working of a "dynamic economy," which compensates their losses by "massive explosions of new jobs and investments . . . occurring elsewhere, in Silicon Valley." That these failures and successes are not happening to the same people or even to the same groups of people is an insight beyond the reach of Mr. Stockman's equipment. By his reasoning, we may readily see that the poverty of the poor is justified by the richness of the rich.

The "free market" idea is the result of a lazy (when not villainous) wish to found the human economy on natural law. The trouble with this is that humans are not *of* nature in the same way that foxes and rabbits are. Humans live artificially, by artifice and by art, by human making, and economics will finally have to be answerable to this. Unbridled economic forces damage *both* nature and human culture.

There are, I suggest, two human laws of economics, very different from the laws, which are in fact both unnatural and inhuman, that govern the "free market":

1. Money must not lie about value. It must not, by inflation or usury, misrepresent the value of necessary work or necessary goods. Those values must not, by any devices of markets or banks, be made subject to monetary manipulation.

2. There must be a decent balance between what people earn and what they pay, and this can be made possible only by control of production. When farmers have to sell on a depressed market and buy on an inflated one, that is death to farmers, death to farming, death to rural communities, death to the soil, and (to put it in urban terms) death to food.

4. *That productivity is a sufficient standard of production.*
By and large, the most popular way of dealing with American agricultural problems has been to praise American agriculture. For decades we have been wandering in a blizzard of production

statistics pouring out of the government, the universities, and the "agribusiness" corporations. No politician's brag would be complete without a tribute to "the American farmer" who is said to be single-handedly feeding seventy-five or one hundred or God knows how many people. American agriculture is fantastically productive, and by now we all ought to know it.

That American agriculture is also fantastically expensive is less known, but it is equally undeniable, even though the costs have not yet entered into the official accounting. The costs are in loss of soil, in loss of farms and farmers, in soil and water pollution, in food pollution, in the decay of country towns and communities, and in the increasing vulnerability of the food supply system. The statistics of productivity alone cannot show these costs. We are nevertheless approaching a "bottom line" that is not on our books.

From an agricultural point of view, a better word than productivity is *thrift*. It is a better word because it implies a fuller accounting. A thrifty person is undoubtedly a productive one, but thriftiness also implies a proper consideration for the means of production. To be thrifty is to take care of things; it is to thrive— that is, to be healthy by being a part of health. One cannot be thrifty alone; one can only be thrifty insofar as one's land, crops, animals, place, and community are thriving.

The great fault of the selective bookkeeping we call "the economy" is that it does not lead to thrift; day by day, we are acting out the plot of a murderous paradox: an "economy" that leads to extravagance. Our great fault as a people is that we do not take care of things. Our economy is such that we say we "cannot afford" to take care of things: Labor is expensive, time is expensive, money is expensive, but materials—the stuff of creation—are so cheap that we cannot afford to take care of them. The wrecking ball is characteristic of our way with materials. We "cannot afford" to log a forest selectively, to mine without destroying topography, or to farm without catastrophic soil erosion.

A production-oriented economy can indeed live in this way, but only so long as production lasts.

Suppose that, foreseeing the inevitable failure of this sort of production, we see that we must assign a value to continuity. If that happens, then our standard of production will have to change; indeed, it will already have changed, for the standard of productivity alone cannot permit us to see that continuity *has* a value. The value of continuity is visible only to thrift.

5. *There are too many farmers.*

This idea has been accepted doctrine in the *offices* of agriculture—in governments, universities, and corporations—ever since World War II. Its history is a remarkable proof of the influence of an idea. In the last forty years, it has aggravated and excused, if indeed it has not caused, one of the most consequential migrations of history: millions of rural people moving from country to city in an exodus that has not ceased from the war's end until now. The motivating force behind this migration, then as now, has been economic ruin on the farm. Today, with hundreds of farm families losing their farms every week, the economists are still saying, as they have said all along, that these people deserve to fail, that they have failed because they are the "least efficient producers," and that America is better off for their failure.

It is apparently easy to say that there are too many farmers, if one is not a farmer. This is not a pronouncement often heard in farm communities, nor have farmers yet been informed of a dangerous surplus of population in the "agribusiness" professions or among the middlemen of the food system. No agricultural economist has yet perceived that there are too many agricultural economists.

The farm-to-city migration has obviously produced advantages to the corporate economy. The absent farmers have had to be replaced by machinery, petroleum, chemicals, credit, and other expensive goods and services from the "agribusiness" economy (which ought not to be confused with the economy of what used to be called farming). But these short-term advantages all imply long-term disadvantages to both country and city. The departure of so many people has seriously weakened rural communities and economies all over the country. That our farmland no longer has enough caretakers is implied by the fact that, as the farming people have departed from the land, the land itself has departed. Our soil erosion rates are now higher than they were in the time of the Dust Bowl.

At the same time, the cities have had to receive a great influx of people unprepared for urban life and unable to cope with it. A friend of mine, a psychologist who has frequently worked with the juvenile courts in a large midwestern city, has told me that a major occupation of the police force there is to keep "the permanently unemployable" confined in their own part of town. Such a circumstance cannot be good for the future of democracy and freedom. One wonders what the authors of our Constitution would have thought of that category, "the permanently unemployable."

Equally important is the question of the sustainability of the urban food supply. The supermarkets are, at present, crammed with food, and the productivity of American agriculture is, at present, enormous. But this is a productivity based on the ruin both of the producers and of the sources of production. City people are not worried about this, apparently, only because they do not know anything about farming. People who know about farming, who know what the farmland requires to remain productive, *are* worried. When topsoil losses exceed the weight of grain harvested by five times (in Iowa) or by twenty times (in the wheatlands of eastern Washington), there is something to worry about.

When the "too many" of the country arrive in the city, they are not called "too many"; in the city they are called "unemployed" or "permanently unemployable." What will happen if the economists ever perceive that there are too many people in the cities? There appear to be only two possibilities: Either they will have to recognize that their earlier diagnosis was a tragic error, or they will conclude that there are too many people in country and city both—and what further inhumanities will be justified by *that* diagnosis?

Both parties in our political dialogue seem to have concluded long ago that the dispossession and disemployment of people by industrial growth are normal and acceptable. The liberals have wished to support these people with welfare giveaways; the conservatives have instructed them to become ambitious and get jobs. Both of these "solutions" are ways of telling the unprivileged to go to hell—the only difference being in the speed with which they are advised to go.

6. *That hand labor is bad.*

This idea, too, is accepted doctrine; indeed, it is one of the chief supports of the doctrine that there are too many farmers. The forced migration of farmers from the farm will be easier on the general conscience if it can be supposed that bankruptcy and dispossession are ways of saving farmers from work that is beneath their dignity.

We can only assume that we are faced with an unquestioned social dogma when so astute a writer as Jane Jacobs can say without blinking that "cotton picking by hand is miserable labor; driving a cotton picker is not" (*Cities and the Wealth of Nations*, 1984). A great many questions have to be asked and answered before this assertion can be allowed to stand. Wes Jackson is certainly right in his insistence that the pleasantness or unpleasantness of farm work depends upon scale—upon the size of the field and the size of the crop. But we also need to know who owns the field, we need to know the experience and the expectations of the workers, and we need to know about the skill of the workers and the quality of the work. After consideration of such matters, we can say that probably *any* farm work is miserable, whether done by hand or by machine, if it is economically desperate—if it does not secure the worker in some stable, decent, rewarding connection to the land worked. We can say that hand work in a small field owned by the worker, who can then expect a decent economic return, is probably less miserable than mechanized work in somebody else's large field. We can suppose with some confidence, moreover, that hand work in the company of family and neighbors might be less miserable than work done alone in the unrelieved noise of a machine.

The fact remains, of course, that millions of hand workers, including the farmers now losing their farms, have been and are being replaced by machines. Many people apparently assume that this process of "labor saving," the substitution of machines for people, can continue indefinitely to the unending betterment of the human lot. But we must continue to ask about the possible necessity, the possible goodness, and the possible inescapability, of hand work.

My own suspicion is that, especially for the private owners of small properties such as farms, hand work may become more necessary as petroleum and other "industrial inputs" become more expensive. Increasingly, too, I think, farmers will find it necessary to substitute their own hand labor in such work as carpentry and machinery repair for more expensive city labor.

I suspect also that a considerable amount of hand work may remain necessary for reasons other than economics. It will continue to be necessary in the best farming because the best farming will continue to rely on the attentiveness and particularity that go with the use of the hands. Animal husbandry will continue to require the use of the hands; so, I think, will much of the work of land restoration, and we are going to have a lot of that to do.

Judging from our epidemic of obesity and other diseases of sedentary life and from the popularity of the various strenuous employments of the "physical fitness movement," the greatest untapped source of usable energy may now be in human bodies. It may become the task of a future economy to give worthy employment to this energy and to reward its use.

A Nation Rich
in Natural Resources

1985

If *economy* means "management of a household," then we have a system of national accounting that bears no resemblance to the national economy whatsoever, for it is not the record of our life at home but the fever chart of our consumption. Our national economy—the health of which might be indicated by our net national product, derived by subtracting our real losses from our real gains—is perhaps a top secret, the existence of which even the government has not yet suspected.

One reason for this is the geographical separation that frequently exists between losses and gains. Agricultural losses occur on the farm and in farming communities, whereas the great gains of agriculture all occur in cities, just as the profits from coal are realized mainly in cities far from where the coal is mined. Almost always the profit is realized by people who are under no pressure or obligation to realize the losses—people, that is, who are so positioned by wealth and power that they need assign no value at all to what is lost. The cost of soil erosion is not deducted from the profit on a packaged beefsteak, just as the loss of forest, topsoil, and human homes on a Kentucky mountainside does not reduce the profit on a ton of coal.

If this peculiar estrangement between losses and gains, between products and their real costs, is institutionalized anywhere, it is in our ubiquitous word, *resource*. One definition of this word is close to the meaning of its Latin root, *resurgere*, to rise again. In this sense, a resource is a dependable (which is to say a constant) supply; a resource rises again as a spring rises, refilling its basin, after a bucket of water has been dipped out. This is what the topsoil and what the human culture of farming can do under the right "household management," the right economy: They replenish themselves and they can last as long as the earth and the sun. The right economy is right insofar as it respects the source, respects the power of the source to resurge, and does not ask too much.

Another, opposite, definition of resource is "means that can be used to advantage." That, I am afraid, is the definition of the word as we now use it. We look upon everything as a resource, even people; the state of Kentucky, for instance, has a Department of Human Resources. With us, a resource is something that has no value until it has been made into something else. Thus, a tree has value only insofar as it can be made into lumber, and our schools, which are more and more understood and justified as dispensers of "job training," are based on the implicit principle that children have no value until they have been made into employees.

Common sense suggests that it is not possible to make a good thing out of a bad thing. We can see that we cannot prepare a good meal from poor food, produce good food from poor soil, maintain good soil without good farming, or have good farming without a good culture—a culture that places a proper value on the proper maintenance of the natural sources, so that the needed supplies are constantly available. Thus, food is a product both natural and cultural, and good cooking must be said to begin with good farming. A good economy would value our bodily nourishment in *all* of its transformations from the topsoil to the dinner table and beyond, for it would place an appropriate value on our excrement, too, and return it to the soil; in a good economy, there would be no such thing as "waste," bodily or otherwise. At every stage of its making, our nourishment would be a finished product in the sense that at every stage it would be brought to a high order of excellence, but at no stage would it be a finished product in the sense of being done with.

We must also notice that as the natural energy approaches human usability, it passes through a declension of forms less and less complex. A potato is less complex than the topsoil, a steak than a steer, a cooked meal than a farm. If, in the human economy, a squash on the table is worth more than a squash in the field, and a squash in the field is worth more than a bushel of soil, that does not mean that food is more valuable than soil; it means simply that we do not know *how* to value the soil. In its complexity and its potential longevity, the soil exceeds our comprehension; we do not know how to place a just market value on it, and we will never learn how. Its value is inestimable; we must value it, beyond whatever price we put on it, by *respecting* it.

The industrial economy, on the other hand, reduces the value of a thing to its market price, and it sets the market price in accordance with the capacity of a thing to be made into another kind of thing. Thus, a farm is valued *only* for its ability to produce marketable livestock and/or crops; livestock and crops are valued *only* insofar as they can be manufactured into groceries; groceries are valued *only* to the extent that they can be sold to consumers. An absolute division is made at every stage of the industrial process between raw materials, to which, as such, we accord no respect at all, and finished products, which we respect only to the extent of their market value. A lot could be said about the quality of the "finish" of these products, but the critical point here is that, in the industrial economy, value in the form of respect is withheld from the source, and value in the form of price is always determined by reference to a *future* usability—nothing is valued for what it is.

But when nothing is valued for what it is, everything is destined to be wasted. Once the values of things refer only to their future usefulness, then an infinite withdrawal of value from the living present has begun. Nothing (and nobody) can then exist that is not theoretically replaceable by something (or somebody) more valuable. The country that we (or some of us) had thought to make our home becomes instead "a nation rich in natural resources"; the good bounty of the land begins its mechanical metamorphosis into junk, garbage, silt, poison, and other forms of "waste."

The inevitable result of such an economy is that no farm or any other usable property can safely be regarded by anyone as a home, no home is ultimately worthy of our loyalty, nothing is ultimately worth doing, and no place or task or person is worth a lifetime's devotion. "Waste," in such an economy, must eventually include several categories of humans—the unborn, the old, "disinvested" farmers, the unemployed, the "unemployable." Indeed, once our homeland, our source, is regarded as a resource, we are all sliding downward toward the ashheap or the dump.

Preserving Wildness

1985

The argument over the proper relation of humanity to nature is becoming, as the sixties used to say, polarized. And the result, as before, is bad talk on both sides. At one extreme are those who sound as if they are entirely in favor of nature; they assume that there is no necessary disjuncture or difference between the human estate and the estate of nature, that human good is in some simple way the same as natural good. They believe, at least in principle, that the biosphere is an egalitarian system, in which all creatures, including humans, are equal in value and have an equal right to live and flourish. These people tend to stand aloof from the issue of the proper human use of nature. Indeed, they have begun to use "stewardship" (meaning the responsible use of nature) as a term of denigration.

At the other extreme are the nature conquerors, who have no patience with an old-fashioned outdoor farm, let alone a wilderness. These people divide all reality into two parts: human good, which they define as profit, comfort, and security; and everything else, which they understand as a stockpile of "natural resources" or "raw materials," which will sooner or later be transformed into human good. The aims of these militant tinkerers invariably manage to be at once unimpeachable and suspect. They wish earnestly, for example, to solve what they call "the problem of hunger"—if it can be done glamorously, comfortably, and profitably. They believe that the ability to do something is the reason to do it. According to a recent press release from the University of Illinois College of Agriculture, researchers there are looking forward to "food production without either farmers or farms." (This is perhaps the first explicit acknowledgment of the program that has been implicit in the work of the land-grant universities for forty or fifty years.)

If I had to choose, I would join the nature extremists against the technology extremists, but this choice seems poor, even assuming that it is possible. I would prefer to stay in the middle, not to avoid taking sides, but because I think the middle *is* a side, as well as the real location of the problem.

The middle, of course, is always rather roomy and bewildering territory, and so I should state plainly the assumptions that define the ground on which I intend to stand:

   1. We live in a wilderness, in which we and our works occupy a tiny space and play a tiny part. We exist under its dispensation and by its tolerance.

   2. This wilderness, the universe, is *somewhat* hospitable to us, but it is also absolutely dangerous to us (it is going to kill us, sooner or later), and we are absolutely dependent upon it.

   3. That we depend upon what we are endangered by is a problem not solvable by "problem solving." It does not have what the nature romantic or the technocrat would regard as a solution. We are not going back to the Garden of Eden, nor are we going to manufacture an Industrial Paradise.

   4. There does exist a possibility that we can live more or less in harmony with our native wilderness; I am betting my life that such a harmony is possible. But I do not believe that it can be achieved simply or easily or that it can ever be perfect, and I am

certain that it can never be made, once and for all, but is the forever unfinished lifework of our species.

5. It is not possible (at least, not for very long) for humans to intend their own good specifically or exclusively. We cannot intend our good, in the long run, without intending the good of our place—which means, ultimately, the good of the world.

6. To use or not to use nature is not a choice that is available to us; we can live only at the expense of other lives. Our choice has rather to do with how and how much to use. This is not a choice that can be decided satisfactorily in principle or in theory; it is a choice intransigently impractical. That is, it must be worked out in local practice because, by necessity, the practice will vary somewhat from one locality to another. There is, thus, no *practical* way that we can intend the good of the world; practice can only be local.

7. If there is no escape from the human use of nature, then human good cannot be simply synonymous with natural good.

What these assumptions describe, of course, is the human predicament. It is a spiritual predicament, for it requires us to be properly humble and grateful; time and again, it asks us to be still and wait. But it is also a practical problem, for it requires us to *do* things.

In going to work on this problem it is a mistake to proceed on the basis of an assumed division or divisibility between nature and humanity, or wildness and domesticity. But it is also a mistake to assume that there is no difference between the natural and the human. If these things could be divided, our life would be far simpler and easier than it is, just as it would be if they were not different. Our problem, exactly, is that the human and the natural are indivisible, and yet are different.

The indivisibility of wildness and domesticity, even within the fabric of human life itself, is easy enough to demonstrate. Our bodily life, to begin at the nearest place, is half wild. Perhaps it is more than half wild, for it is dependent upon reflexes, instincts, and appetites that we do not cause or intend and that we cannot, or had better not, stop. We live, partly, because we are domestic creatures—that is, we participate in our human economy to the extent that we "make a living"; we are able, with variable success, to discipline our appetites and instincts in order to produce this artifact, this human living. And yet it is equally true that we breathe and our hearts beat and we survive as a species because we are wild.

The same is true of a healthy human economy as it branches upward out of the soil. The topsoil, to the extent that it is fertile, is wild; it is a dark wilderness, ultimately unknowable, teeming with wildlife. A forest or a crop, no matter how intentionally husbanded by human foresters or farmers, will be found to be healthy precisely to the extent that it is wild—able to collaborate with earth, air, light, and water in the way common to plants before humans walked the earth. We know from experience that we can increase our domestic demands upon plants so far that we force them into kinds of failure that wild plants do not experience.

Breeders of domestic animals, likewise, know that, when a breeding program is too much governed by human intention, by economic considerations, or by fashion, uselessness is the result. Size or productivity, for instance, will be gained at the cost of health, vigor, or reproductive ability. In other words, so-called domestic animals must remain half wild, or more than half, because they are creatures of nature. Humans are intelligent enough to select for a type of creature; they are not intelligent enough to *make* a creature. Their efforts to make an entirely domestic animal, like their efforts to make an entirely domestic human, are doomed to failure because they do not have and undoubtedly are never going to have the full set of production standards for the making of creatures. From a human point of view, then, creature making is wild. The effort to make plants, animals, and humans ever more governable by human intentions is continuing with more determination and more violence than ever, but that does not mean that it is nearer to success. It means only that we are increasing the violence and the magnitude of the expectable reactions.

To be divided against nature, against wildness, then, is a human disaster because it is to be divided against ourselves. It confines our identity as creatures entirely within the bounds of our own understanding, which is invariably a mistake because it is invariably reductive. It reduces our largeness, our mystery, to a petty and sickly comprehensibility.

But to say that we are not divided and not dividable from nature is not to say that there is no difference between us and the other creatures. Human nature partakes of nature, participates in it, is dependent on it, and yet is different from it. We feel the difference as discomfort or difficulty or danger. Nature is not easy to live with. It is hard to have rain on your cut hay, or floodwater over your cropland, or coyotes in your sheep; it is hard when nature does not respect your intentions, and she never does exactly respect them. Moreover, such problems belong to all of us, to the human lot. Humans who do not experience them are exempt only because they are paying (or underpaying) other humans such as farmers to deal with nature on their behalf. Further, it is not just agriculture-dependent humanity that has had to put up with natural dangers and frustrations; these have been the lot of hunting and gathering societies also, and the wild creatures do not always live comfortably or easily with nature either.

But humans differ most from other creatures in the extent to which they must be *made* what they are—that is, in the extent to which they are artifacts of their culture. It is true that what we might as well call culture does go into the making of some birds and animals, but this teaching is so much less than the teaching that makes a human as to be almost a different thing. To take a creature who is biologically a human and to make him or her fully human is a task that requires many years (some of us sometimes fear that it requires more than a lifetime), and this long effort of human making is necessary, I think, because of our power. In the hierarchy of power among the earth's creatures, we are at the top, and we have been growing stronger for a long time. We are now, to ourselves, incomprehensibly powerful, capable of doing more damage than floods, storms, volcanoes, and earthquakes. And so it is more important than ever that we should have cultures capable of making us into humans—creatures capable of prudence, justice, fortitude, temperance, and the other virtues. For our history reveals that, stripped of the restraints, disciplines, and ameliorations of culture, humans are not "natural," not "thinking animals" or "naked apes," but monsters—indiscriminate and insatiable killers and destroyers. We differ from other creatures, partly, in our susceptibility to monstrosity. It is perhaps for this reason that, in the wake of the great wars of our century, we have seen poets such as T. S. Eliot, Ezra Pound, and David Jones making an effort to reweave the tattered garment of culture and to reestablish the cultural tasks, which are, as Pound put it, "To know the histories / to know good from evil / And know whom to trust." And we see, if we follow Pound a little further, that the recovery of culture involves, leads to, or is the recovery of nature:

> the trees rise
> and there is a wide sward between them
> . . . myrrh and olibanum on the altar stone
> giving perfume,
>   and where was nothing
> now is furry assemblage
>   and in the boughs now are voices . . .

In the recovery of culture *and* nature is the knowledge of how to farm well, how to preserve, harvest, and replenish the forests, how to make, build, and use, return and restore. In this *double* recovery, which is the recovery of our humanity, is the hope that the domestic and the wild can exist together in lasting harmony.

This doubleness of allegiance and responsibility, difficult as it always is, confusing as it sometimes is, apparently is inescapable.

A culture that does not measure itself by nature, by an understanding of its debts to nature, becomes destructive of nature and thus of itself. A culture that does not measure itself by its own best work and the best work of other cultures (the determination of which is its unending task) becomes destructive of itself and thus of nature.

Harmony is one phase, the good phase, of the inescapable dialogue between culture and nature. In this phase, humans consciously and conscientiously ask of their work: Is this good for us? Is this good for our place? And the questioning and answering in this phase is minutely particular: It can occur only with reference to particular artifacts, events, places, ecosystems, and neighborhoods. When the cultural side of the dialogue becomes too theoretical or abstract, the other phase, the bad one, begins. Then the conscious, responsible questions are not asked; acts begin to be committed and things to be made on their own terms for their own sakes, culture deteriorates, and nature retaliates.

The awareness that we are slowly growing into now is that the earthly wildness that we are so complexly dependent upon is at our mercy. It has become, in a sense, our artifact because it can only survive by a human understanding and forbearance that we now must make. The only thing we have to preserve nature with is culture; the only thing we have to preserve wildness with is domesticity.

To me, this means simply that we are not safe in assuming that we can preserve wildness by making wilderness preserves. Those of us who see that wildness and wilderness need to be preserved are going to have to understand the dependence of these things upon our domestic economy and our domestic behavior. If we do not have an economy capable of valuing in particular terms the durable good of localities and communities, then we are not going to be able to preserve anything. We are going to have to see that, if we want our forests to last, then we must make wood products that last, for our forests are more threatened by shoddy workmanship than by clear-cutting or by fire. Good workmanship—that is, careful, considerate, and loving work—requires us to think considerately of the whole process, natural and cultural, involved in the making of wooden artifacts, because the good worker does not share the industrial contempt for "raw material." The good worker loves the board before it becomes a table, loves the tree before it yields the board, loves the forest before it gives up the tree. The good worker understands that a badly made artifact is both an insult to its user and a danger to its source. We could say, then, that good forestry begins with the respectful husbanding of the forest that we call stewardship and ends with well-made tables and chairs and houses, just as good agriculture begins with stewardship of the fields and ends with good meals.

In other words, conservation is going to prove increasingly futile and increasingly meaningless if its proscriptions are not answered positively by an economy that rewards and enforces good use. I would call this a loving economy, for it would strive to place a proper value on all the materials of the world, in all their metamorphoses from soil and water, air and light to the finished goods of our towns and households, and I think that the only effective motive for this would be a particularizing love for local things, rising out of local knowledge and local allegiance.

Our present economy, by contrast, does not account for affection at all, which is to say that it does not account for value. It is simply a description of the career of money as it preys upon both nature and human society. Apparently because our age is so manifestly unconcerned for the life of the spirit, many people conclude that it places an undue value on material things. But that cannot be so, for people who valued material things would take care of them and would care for the sources of them. We could argue that an age that *properly* valued and cared for material things would be an age properly spiritual. In my part of the country, the Shakers, "unworldly" as they were, were the true materialists, for they truly valued materials. And they valued them in the only way that such things *can* be valued in practice:

by good workmanship, both elegant and sound. The so-called materialism of our own time is, by contrast, at once indifferent to spiritual concerns and insatiably destructive of the material world. And I would call our economy, not materialistic, but abstract, intent upon the subversion of both spirit and matter by abstractions of value and of power. In such an economy, it is impossible to value anything that one *has*. What one has (house or job, spouse or car) is only valuable insofar as it can be exchanged for what one believes that one wants—a limitless economic process based upon boundless dissatisfaction.

Now that the practical processes of industrial civilization have become so threatening to humanity and to nature, it is easy for us, or for some of us, to see that practicality needs to be made subject to spiritual values and spiritual measures. But we must not forget that it is also necessary for spirituality to be responsive to practical questions. For human beings the spiritual and the practical are, and should be, inseparable. Alone, practicality becomes dangerous; spirituality, alone, becomes feeble and pointless. Alone, either becomes dull. Each is the other's discipline, in a sense, and in good work the two are joined.

"The dignity of toil is undermined when its necessity is gone," Kathleen Raine says, and she is right. It is an insight that we dare not ignore, and I would emphasize that it applies to *all* toil. What is not needed is frivolous. Everything depends on our right relation to necessity—and therefore on our right definition of necessity. In defining our necessity, we must be careful to discount the subsidies, the unrepaid borrowings, from nature that have so far sustained industrial civilization: the "cheap" fossil fuels and ores; the forests that have been cut down and not replanted; the virgin soils of much of the world, whose fertility has not been replenished.

And so, though I am trying to unspecialize the idea and the job of preserving wildness, I am not against wilderness preservation. I am only pointing out, as the Reagan administration has done, that the wildernesses we are trying to preserve are standing squarely in the way of our present economy, and that the wildernesses cannot survive if our economy does not change.

The reason to preserve wilderness is that we need it. We need wilderness of all kinds, large and small, public and private. We need to go now and again into places where our work is disallowed, where our hopes and plans have no standing. We need to come into the presence of the unqualified and mysterious formality of Creation. And I would agree with Edward Abbey that we need as well some tracts of what he calls "absolute wilderness," which "through general agreement none of us enters at all."

We need wilderness also because wildness—nature—is one of our indispensable studies. We need to understand it as our source and preserver, as an essential measure of our history and behavior, and as the ultimate definer of our possibilities. There are, I think, three questions that must be asked with respect to a human economy in any given place:

1. What is here?
2. What will nature permit us to do here?
3. What will nature help us to do here?

The second and third questions are obviously the ones that would define agendas of practical research and of work. If we do not work with and within natural tolerances, then we will not be permitted to work for long. It is plain enough, for example, that if we use soil fertility faster than nature can replenish it, we are proposing an end that we do not desire. And to ignore the possibility of help from nature makes farming, for example, too expensive for farmers—as we are seeing. It may make life too expensive for humans.

But the second and third questions are ruled by the first. They cannot be answered—they cannot intelligently be asked—until the first has been answered. And yet the first question has not been answered, or asked, so far as I know, in the whole history of the American economy. All the great changes, from the Indian wars and the opening of agricultural frontiers to the inauguration of genetic engineering, have been made without a backward look and in ignorance of whereabouts. Our response to the forest and the prairie that covered our present fields was to get them out of the way as soon as possible. And the obstructive human populations of Indians and "inefficient" or small farmers have been dealt with in the same spirit. We have never known what we were doing because we have never known what we were *un*doing. We cannot know what we are doing until we know what nature would be doing if we were doing nothing. And that is why we need small native wildernesses widely dispersed over the countryside as well as large ones in spectacular places.

However, to say that wilderness and wildness are indispensable to us, indivisible from us, is not to say that we can find sufficient standards for our life and work in nature. To suggest that, for humans, there is a simple equation between "natural" and "good" is to fall prey immediately to the cynics who love to point out that, after all, "everything is natural." They are, of course, correct. Nature provides bountifully for her children, but, as we would now say, she is also extremely permissive. If her children want to destroy one another entirely or to commit suicide, that is all right with her. There is nothing, after all, more natural than the extinction of species; the extinction of *all* species, we must assume, would also be perfectly natural.

Clearly, if we want to argue for the existence of the world as we know it, we will have to find some way of qualifying and supplementing this relentless criterion of "natural." Perhaps we can do so only by a reaffirmation of a lesser kind of naturalness—that of self-interest. Certainly human self-interest has much wickedness to answer for, and we are living in just fear of it; nevertheless, we must take care not to condemn it absolutely. After all, we value this passing work of nature that we call "the natural world," with its graceful plenty of animals and plants, precisely because *we* need it and love it and want it for a home.

We are creatures obviously subordinate to nature, dependent upon a wild world that we did not make. And yet we are joined to that larger nature by our own nature, a part of which is our self-interest. A common complaint nowadays is that humans think the world is "anthropocentric," or human-centered. I understand the complaint; the assumptions of so-called anthropocentrism often result in gross and dangerous insubordination. And yet I don't know how the human species can avoid some version of self-centeredness; I don't know how any species can. An earthworm, I think, is living in an earthworm-centered world; the thrush who eats the earthworm is living in a thrush-centered world; the hawk who eats the thrush is living in a hawk-centered world. Each creature, that is, does what is necessary in its own behalf, and is domestic in its own *domus* or home.

Humans differ from earthworms, thrushes, and hawks in their capacity to do more—in modern times, a great deal more—in their own behalf than is necessary. Moreover, the vast majority of humans in the industrial nations are guilty of this extravagance. One of the oldest human arguments is over the question of how much is necessary. How much must humans do in their own behalf in order to be fully human? The number and variety of the answers ought to notify us that we never have known for sure, and yet we have the disquieting suspicion that, almost always, the honest answer has been "less."

We have no way to work at this question, it seems to me, except by perceiving that, in order to have the world, we must share it, both with each other and with other creatures, which is immediately complicated by the further perception that, in order to live in the world, we must use it somewhat at the expense of other creatures. We must acknowledge both the centrality and the limits of our self-interest. One can hardly imagine a tougher situation.

But in the recognition of the difficulty of our situation is a kind of relief, for it makes us give up the hope that a solution can be found in a simple preference for humanity over nature or nature over humanity. The only solutions we have ahead of us will need to be worked for and worked out. They will have to be practical solutions, resulting in good local practice. There is work to do that can be done.

As we undertake this work, perhaps the greatest immediate danger lies in our dislike of ourselves as a species. This is an understandable dislike—we are justly afraid of ourselves—but we are nevertheless obliged to think and act out of a proper self-interest and a genuine self-respect as human beings. Otherwise, we will allow our dislike and fear of ourselves to justify further abuses of one another and the world. We must come to terms with the fact that it is not natural to be disloyal to one's own kind.

For these reasons, there is great danger in the perception that "there are too many people," whatever truth may be in it, for this is a premise from which it is too likely that somebody, sooner or later, will proceed to a determination of *who* are the surplus. If we conclude that there are too many, it is hard to avoid the further conclusion that there are some we do not need. But how many do we need, and which ones? Which ones, now apparently unnecessary, may turn out later to be indispensable? We do not know; it is a part of our mystery, our wildness, that we do not know.

I would argue that, at least for us in the United States, the conclusion that "there are too many people" is premature, not because I know that there are *not* too many people, but because I do not think we are prepared to come to such a conclusion. I grant that questions about population size need to be asked, but they are not the *first* questions that need to be asked.

The "population problem," initially, should be examined as a problem, not of quantity, but of pattern. Before we conclude that we have too many people, we must ask if we have people who are misused, people who are misplaced, or people who are abusing the places they have. The facts of most immediate importance may be, not how many we are, but where we are and what we are doing. At any rate, the attempt to solve our problems by reducing

our numbers may be a distraction from the overriding population statistic of our time: that *one* human with a nuclear bomb
and the will to use it is 100 percent too many. I would argue that
it is not human fecundity that is overcrowding the world so much
as technological multipliers of the power of individual humans.
The worst disease of the world now is probably the ideology of
technological heroism, according to which more and more people willingly cause large-scale effects that they do not foresee and
that they cannot control. This is the ideology of the professional
class of the industrial nations—a class whose allegiance to communities and places has been dissolved by their economic motives
and by their educations. These are people who will go anywhere
and jeopardize anything in order to assure the success of their
careers.

We may or may not have room for more people, but it is certain that we do not have more room for technological heroics. We
do not need any more thousand-dollar solutions to ten-dollar
problems or million-dollar solutions to thousand-dollar problems—or multibillion-dollar solutions where there was never a
problem at all. We have no way to compute the inhabitability of
our places; we cannot weigh or measure the pleasures we take in
them; we cannot say how many dollars domestic tranquillity is
worth. And yet we must now learn to bear in mind the memory of
communities destroyed, disfigured, or made desolate by technological events, as well as the memory of families dispossessed,
displaced, and impoverished by "labor-saving" machines. The
issue of human obsolescence may be more urgent for us now than
the issue of human population.

The population issue thus leads directly to the issue of proportion and scale. What is the proper amount of power for a human
to use? What are the proper limits of human enterprise? How
may these proprieties be determined? Such questions may seem
inordinately difficult, but that is because we have gone too long
without asking them. One of the fundamental assumptions of

industrial economics has been that such questions are outmoded and that we need never ask them again. The failure of that assumption now requires us to reconsider the claims of wildness and to renew our understanding of the old ideas of propriety and harmony.

When we propose that humans should learn to behave properly with respect to nature so as to place their domestic economy harmoniously upon and within the sustaining and surrounding wilderness, then we make possible a sort of landscape criticism. Then we can see that it is not primarily the number of people inhabiting a landscape that determines the propriety of the ratio and the relation between human domesticity and wildness, but it is the way the people divide the landscape and use it. We can see that it is the landscape of monoculture in which both nature and humanity are most at risk. We feel the human fragility of the huge one-class housing development, just as we feel the natural fragility of the huge one-crop field.

Looking at the monocultures of industrial civilization, we yearn with a kind of homesickness for the humanness and the naturalness of a highly diversified, multipurpose landscape, democratically divided, with many margins. The margins are of the utmost importance. They are the divisions between holdings, as well as between kinds of work and kinds of land. These margins—lanes, streamsides, wooded fencerows, and the like—are always freeholds of wildness, where limits are set on human intention. Such places are hospitable to the wild lives of plants and animals and to the wild play of human children. They enact, within the bounds of human domesticity itself, a human courtesy toward the wild that is one of the best safeguards of designated tracts of true wilderness. This is the landscape of harmony, safer far for life of all kinds than the landscape of monoculture. And we should not neglect to notice that, whereas the monocultural landscape is totalitarian in tendency, the landscape of harmony is democratic and free.

A Good Farmer
of the Old School

At the 1982 Draft Horse Sale in Columbus, Ohio, Maury Telleen summoned me over to the group of horsemen with whom he was talking: "Come here," he said, "I want you to hear this." One of those horsemen was Lancie Clippinger, and what Maury wanted me to hear was the story of Lancie's corn crop of the year before.

The story, which Lancie obligingly told again, was as interesting to me as Maury had expected it to be. Lancie, that year, had planted forty acres of corn; he had also bred forty gilts that he had raised so that their pigs would be ready to feed when the corn would be ripe. The gilts produced 360 pigs, an average of nine per head. When the corn was ready for harvest, Lancie divided off a strip of the field with an electric fence and turned in the 360 shoats. After the shoats had fed on that strip for a while, Lancie opened a new strip for them. He then picked the strip where they had just fed. In that way, he fattened his 360 shoats and also harvested all the corn he needed for his other stock.

The shoats brought $40,000. Lancie's expenses had been for seed corn, 275 pounds of fertilizer per acre, and one quart per acre of herbicide. He did not say what the total costs amounted to, but it was clear enough that his net income from the forty acres of corn had been high, in a year when the corn itself would have brought perhaps two dollars a bushel.

At the end of the story, I remember, Lancie and Maury had a conversation that went about like this:

"Do you farrow your sows in a farrowing house?"

"No."

"Oh, you do it in huts, then?"

"No, I have a field I turn them out in. It has plenty of shade and water. And I see them every day."

Here was an intelligent man, obviously, who knew the value of doing his own thinking and paying attention, who understood clearly that the profit is in the difference between costs and earnings, and who proceeded directly to minimize his costs. In a time when hog farmers often spend many thousands of dollars on highly specialized housing and equipment, Lancie's "hog operation" consisted almost entirely of hogs. His principle outlays otherwise were for the farm itself and for fencing. But what struck me most, I think, was the way he had employed nature and the hogs themselves to his own advantage. The bred sows needed plenty of shade, water, and room for exercise; Lancie provided those things, and nature did the rest. He also supplied his own care and attention, which came free; they did not have to be purchased at an inflated cost from an industrial supplier. And then, instead of harvesting his corn mechanically, hauling it, storing it, grinding it, and hauling it to his shoats, he let the shoats harvest and grind it for themselves. He had the use of the whole hog, whereas in a "confinement operation," the hog's feet, teeth, and eyes have virtually no use and produce no profit.

At the next Columbus Sale, I hunted Lancie up, and again we spent a long time talking. We talked about draft horses, of course, but also about milk cows and dairying. And that part of our conversation interested me about as much as the hog story had the year before. What so impressed me was Lancie's belief that there is a limit to the number of cows that a dairy farmer can manage well; he thought the maximum number to be about twenty-five: "If a fellow milks twenty-five cows, he'll *see* them all." If he milks more than that, Lancie said, even though he may touch them all, he will not *see* them all. As in Lancie's account of his corn crop and the 360 shoats, the emphasis here was on the importance of seeing, of paying attention. That this is important economically, he made clear in something he said to me later: "You can take care of twenty or twenty-five cows and do it right. More, you're overlooking things that cost you money." It is necessary, Lancie thinks, to limit the scale of operation, not only in dairying, but in all other enterprises on the farm because proper scale permits a correct balance between work and care. The distinction he was making, it seemed to me, was between work, as it has been understood traditionally on the farm, and processing, as it is understood in industry.

Those two conversations stayed in my mind, proving useful many times in my effort to understand the troubles developing in our agricultural economy. I knew that Lancie Clippinger was one of the best farmers of the old school, and I promised myself that I would visit him at his farm, which I was finally able to do in October 1985.

The farm is on somewhat rolling land, surrounded by wood-lots and brushy fencerows, so that it has a little of the feeling of a large forest clearing. There are 175 acres, of which about 135 are cropped; the rest is in permanent pasture and woods. Although conveniently close to the state road, the farm is at the end of a lane, set off to itself. It is pretty and quiet, a pleasant place to live and to farm, as well as to visit. Lancie and his wife, Verna Bell, bought the place and moved there in the fall of 1971.

When my wife and I drove into the yard, Kathy, one of Lancie's granddaughters, who had evidently been watching for us, came out of the house to meet us. She took us out through the barn lot to a granary where Lancie, his son Keith, and Sherri, another granddaughter, were sacking some oats. We waited, talking with Kathy, while they finished the job, and then we went with Lancie and Keith to look at the horses.

Lancie keeps only geldings, buying them at sales as weanlings, raising and breaking them, selling them, and then replacing them with new colts. When we were there, he had nine head: a pair of black Percherons, a handsome crossbred bay with black mane and tail, and six Belgians. Though he prefers Percherons, he does not specialize; at the sales, his only aim is to buy "colts that look like they'll grow into good big horses." He wants them big because the big ones bring the best prices, but, like nearly all draft horse people who use their horses, he would rather have smaller ones—fifteen hundred pounds or so—if he were keeping them only to work.

The horses he led out for us were in prime condition, and he had been right about them: They had, sure enough, grown into good big ones. These horses may be destined for pulling contests and show hitches, but while they are at Lancie's they put in a lot of time at farm work—they work their way through school, you might say. Like so many farmers of his time, Lancie once made the change from horses to tractors, but with him this did not last long. He was without horses "for a little while" in the seventies, and after that he began to use them again. Now he uses the horses for "just about everything" except cutting and baling his hay and picking his corn. Last spring he used his big tractor only two days. The last time he went to use it, it wouldn't start, and he left it sitting in the shed; it was still sitting there at the time of our visit.

Part of the justification for the return to the use of horses is economic. When he was doing all his work with tractors, Lancie's fuel bill was $6,000 a year; now it is about $2,000. Since the horses themselves are a profit-making enterprise on this farm, the $4,000 they save on fuel is money in the bank. But the economic reason is not the only one: "Pleasure," Lancie says, "is a big part of it." At the year's end, his bank account will show a difference that the horses have made, but day by day his reason for working them is that he *likes* to.

He does not need nine horses in order to do his farming. He has so many because he needs to keep replacements on hand for the horses he sells. He aims, he says, to sell "two or three or four horses every year." To farm his 175 acres, he needs only four good geldings, although he would probably like to keep five, in case he needed a spare. With four horses on his grain drill, he can plant fifteen or twenty acres in a day. He uses four horses also on an eight-foot tandem disk and a springtooth harrow, and he can plant twelve or fifteen acres of corn a day "and not half try."

In plowing, he goes by the old rule of thumb that you can plow an acre per horse per day, provided the horses are in hard condition. "If you start at seven in the morning and stay there the way you ought to," he says, "you can plow three acres a day with three horses." That is what he does, and he does it with a walking plow because, he says, it is easier to walk than to ride. That, of course, is hardly a popular opinion, and Lancie is amused by the surprise it sometimes causes.

One spring, he says, after he had started plowing, he ordered some lime. When the trucker brought the first load, he stopped by the house to ask where to spread it. Mrs. Clippinger told him that Lancie was plowing, and pointed out to the field where Lancie could be seen walking in the furrow behind his plow and team. The trucker was astonished: "Even the *Amish* ride!"

In 1936, Lancie remembers, he plowed a hundred acres, sixty of them in sod, with two horses, Bob and Joe. Together, that team weighed about thirty-five hundred pounds. They were blacks. Lancie had been logging with them before he started plowing, and they were in good shape, ready to go. They plowed two acres a day, six days a week, for nearly nine weeks. It is the sort of thing, one guesses, that could have been done only because all the conditions were right: a strong young man, a tough team, a good season. "Looked like, back then, there wasn't any bad weather," Lancie says, laughing. "You could work all the time."

This farmer's extensive use of live horsepower is possible because his farm is the right size for it and because a sensible rotation of crops both reduces the acreage to be plowed each year and distributes the other field work so that not too much needs to be done at any one time. Of the farm's 135 arable acres, approximately fifty-five will be in corn, forty in oats, and forty in alfalfa. Each of the crops will be grown on the same land two years in order to avoid buying alfalfa seed every year.

The two-year-old alfalfa, turned under, supplies enough nitrogen for the first year of corn. In the second year, the corn crop receives a little commercial nitrogen. The routine application of fertilizer on the corn is 275 pounds per acre of 10-10-20, drilled into the row with the planter. The oats are fertilized at the same rate as the corn, while the alfalfa field, because Lancie sells quite a bit of hay, receives 600 pounds per acre of 3-14-42 in two applications every year. The land is limed at a rate of two tons per acre every time it is plowed. Otherwise, for fertilization Lancie depends on manure from his cattle and horses. "That's what counts," he says. It counts because it pays but does not cost. He usually has enough manure to cover his corn ground every year.

This system of management has not only maintained the productive capacity of the farm but has greatly improved it. Fourteen years ago, when Lancie began on it, the place was farmed out. The previous farmer had plowed it all and planted it all in corn year after year. When the farm sold in the fall of 1971, the corn crop, which was still standing, was bought by a neighboring farmer, who found it not worth picking. Lancie plowed it under the next spring. In order to have a corn crop that first year, he used 900 pounds of fertilizer to the acre—300 pounds of nitrogen and 600 of "straight analysis." After that, when his rotations and other restorative practices had been established, he went to his present rate of 275 pounds of 10-10-20. The resulting rates of production speak well for good care: The corn has made 150 bushels per acre, Lancie says, "for a long time"; this year his oats made 109 bushels per acre, and he also harvested 11,000 fifty-pound bales of alfalfa hay from a forty-acre field (a per-acre yield of about seven tons) and sold 4,800 bales for $12,000.

In addition to seed and fertilizer, Lancie purchases some insecticide and herbicide. This year his alfalfa was sprayed once for weevils, and he used a half-pint of 2-4-D per acre on his corn. The 2-4-D, he says, would not have been necessary if he had cultivated four times instead of twice. Using the chemical saved two cultivations that would have interfered with hay harvest.

What is most significant about Lancie's management of his crops is that it gives his farm a degree of independence that is unusual in these times. The farm, first of all, is ordered and used according to its own nature and carrying capacity, not according to the dictates of farm policy, expert advice, or fluctuations of the economy. The possibility of solving one's economic problems by production alone is not, in Lancie's opinion, a good possibility. If you are losing money on the corn you produce, he points out, the more you produce the more you lose. That so many farmers continue to compensate for low grain prices by increasing production, at great cost to their farms and to themselves, is a sort of wonder to him. "The cheaper it is, the more they plow," he says. "I don't know what they mean." His own farm, by contrast, grows approximately the same acreages of the same crops every year, not because that is what the economy supposedly demands, but because that is what the land can produce at the least cost for the longest time.

Since the farm itself is so much the source of its own fertility and operating energy, Lancie's use of purchased supplies can be minimal, selective, and nonaddictive. Because his cropping pattern and system of management are sound, Lancie can buy these things to suit his convenience. His total expense for 2-4-D for his corn this year, for example, was fifty-six dollars—a very small price to pay in order to have his hands and his mind free at haying time. The point, I think, is that he had a choice: He could choose to do what made the most sense. A further point is that he can quit using chemicals and purchased fertilizer if it ever makes economic sense to do so. As a farmer, he is not addicted to these things.

The conventional industrial farmer, on the other hand, is too often the prisoner of his own technology and methods and has no choice but to continue to do as he has done, whatever the disadvantages. A farmer who has no fences cannot turn hogs in to harvest his corn when prices are low. A farmer who has invested heavily in a farrowing house and all the equipment that goes with it is stuck with that investment. If, for some reason, it ceases to be profitable for him to produce feeder pigs, he still has the farrowing house, which is good for little else, and perhaps a debt on it as well. Thus, mental paralysis and economic slavery can be instituted on a farm by the farmer's technological choices.

One of the main results of Lancie Clippinger's independence is versatility, enabling him to take advantage quickly of opportunities as they appear. Because he has invested in no expensive specialized equipment, he can change his ways to suit his wishes or his circumstances. That he did well raising and finishing shoats one year does not mean that he must continue to raise them. Last year, for instance, he thought there was money to be made on skinny sows. He bought sixty-two at $100 a head, turned them into his cornfield, and, while they ate, he picked. "We all worked together," he says. The sows did a nearly perfect job of gleaning the field, and they brought $200 a head when he sold them.

There is a direct economic payoff in this freedom of choice: It pays to be able to choose to substitute a team of horses for a tractor, or manure for fertilizer, or cultivation for herbicides. When you cultivate a field of corn, as Lancie says, "you're selling your labor"; in other words, you ensure a relation between production and consumption that is proper because it makes sound economic sense. If the farmer does not achieve that proper relation on his farm, he will be a victim. When Lancie prepares his ground with plow and harrow and cultivates his crop instead of buying chemicals, he is a producer, not a consumer; he is selling his labor, not buying an expensive substitute for labor. Moreover, when he does this with a team of horses instead of buying fuel, he is selling his team's labor, not paying for an expensive substitute. When he uses his own corn, oats, and hay to replace petroleum, he is selling those feeds for a far higher return than he could get on the market. He and his horses are functioning, in effect, as solar converters, making usable and profitable the free sunlight that falls onto the farm. They are producing at home the energy, weed control, and fertility that other farmers are going broke trying to pay for.

The industrial farmer consumes more than he produces and is a captive consumer of the suppliers who have prospered by the ruination of such farmers. So far as the national economy is concerned, this kind of farmer exists only to provide cheap food and to enrich the agribusiness corporations, at his own expense.

Sometimes Lancie's intelligent methods and his habit of paying attention yield unexpected dividends. The year after he hogged down the forty acres of corn with the 360 shoats, the field was covered with an excellent stand of alsike clover. "It was pretty," Lancie says, but he didn't know where it came from. He asked around in the neighborhood and discovered that the field had been in alsike seventeen years before. The seed had lain in the ground all that time, waiting for conditions to be right, and somehow the hogs had made them right. Thus, that year's very profitable corn harvest, which had been so well planned, resulted in a valuable gift that nobody had planned—or could have planned. There is no recipe, so far as I know, for making such a thing happen. Obviously, though, a certain eligibility is required. It happened on Lancie's farm undoubtedly because he is the kind of farmer he is. If he had been plowing the whole farm every year and planting it all in corn, as his predecessor had, such a thing would not have happened.

It is care, obviously, that makes the difference. The farm gives gifts because it is given a chance to do so; it is not overcropped or overused. One of Lancie's kindnesses to his farm is his regular rotation of his crops; another is his keeping of livestock, which gives him not only the advantages I have already described but also permits him to make appropriate use of land not suited to row cropping. Like many farms in the allegedly flat corn belt,

Lancie's farm includes some land that should be kept permanently grassed, and on his farm, unlike many, it *is* kept permanently grassed. He can afford this because he can make good use of it that way, without damaging it, for these thirty or so acres give him five hundred bales of bluegrass hay early in the year and, after that, months of pasture, at the cost only of a second clipping. The crop on that land does not need to be planted or cultivated, and it is harvested by the animals; it is therefore the cheapest feed on the place.

Lancie Clippinger is as much in the business of growing crops and making money on them as any other farmer. But he is also in the business of making sense—making sense, that is, for himself, not for the oil, chemical, and equipment companies, or for the banks. He is taking his own advice, and his advice comes from his experience and the experience of farmers like him, not from experts who are not farmers. For those reasons, Lancie Clippinger is doing all right. He is farming well and earning a living by it in a time when many farmers are farming poorly and making money for everybody but themselves.

"I don't know what they mean," he says. "You'd think some in the bunch would use their heads a *little* bit."

A Defense of
the Family Farm

1986

Defending the family farm is like defending the Bill of Rights or the Sermon on the Mount or Shakespeare's plays. One is amazed at the necessity for defense, and yet one agrees gladly, knowing that the family farm is both eminently defensible and a part of the definition of one's own humanity. But having agreed to this defense, one remembers uneasily that there has been a public clamor in defense of the family farm throughout all the years of its decline—that, in fact, "the family farm" has become a political catchword, like democracy and Christianity, and much evil has been done in its name.

Several careful distinctions are therefore necessary. What I shall mean by the term "family farm" is a farm small enough to be farmed by a family and one that *is* farmed by a family, perhaps with a small amount of hired help. I shall *not* mean a farm that is owned by a family and worked by other people. The family farm is both the home and the workplace of the family that owns it.

By the verb "farm," I do not mean just the production of marketable crops but also the responsible maintenance of the health and usability of the place while it is in production. A family farm is one that is properly cared for by its family.

Furthermore, the term "family farm" implies longevity in the connection between family and farm. A family farm is not a farm that a family has bought on speculation and is only occupying and using until it can be profitably sold. Neither, strictly speaking, is it a farm that a family has newly bought, though, depending on the intentions of the family, we may be able to say that such a farm is *potentially* a family farm. This suggests that we may have to think in terms of ranks or degrees of family farms. A farm that has been in the same family for three generations may rank higher as a family farm than a farm that has been in a family only one generation; it may have a higher degree of familiness or familiarity than the one-generation farm. Such distinctions have a practical usefulness to the understanding of agriculture, and, as I hope to show, there are rewards of longevity that do not accrue only to the farm family.

I mentioned the possibility that a family farm might use a small amount of hired help. This greatly complicates matters, and I wish it were possible to say, simply, that a family farm is farmed with family labor. But it seems important to allow for the possibility of supplementing family labor with wagework or some form of sharecropping. Not only may family labor become insufficient as a result, say, of age or debility but also an equitable system of wage earning or sharecropping would permit unpropertied families to earn their way to farm ownership. The critical points, in defining "family farm," are that the amount of non-family labor should be small and that it should supplement, not replace, family labor. On a family farm, the family members are workers, not overseers. If a family on a family farm does require supplementary labor, it seems desirable that the hired help should live on the place and work year-round; the idea of a family farm is jeopardized by supposing that the farm family might be simply the guardians or maintainers of crops planted and harvested by seasonal workers. These requirements, of course, imply both small scale and diversity.

Finally, I think we must allow for the possibility that a family farm might be very small or marginal and that it might not entirely support its family. In such cases, though the economic return might be reduced, the *values* of the family-owned and family-worked small farm are still available both to the family and to the nation.

The idea of the family farm, as I have just defined it, is conformable in every way to the idea of good farming—that is, farming that does not destroy either farmland or farm people. The two ideas may, in fact, be inseparable. If family farming and good farming are as nearly synonymous as I suspect they are, that is because of a law that is well understood, still, by most farmers but that has been ignored in the colleges, offices, and corporations of agriculture for thirty-five or forty years. The law reads something like this: Land that is in human use must be lovingly used; it requires intimate knowledge, attention, and care.

The practical meaning of this law (to borrow an insight from Wes Jackson[1]) is that there is a ratio between eyes and acres, between farm size and farm hands, that is correct. We know that this law is unrelenting—that, for example, one of the meanings of our current high rates of soil erosion is that we do not have enough farmers; we have enough farmers to use the land but not enough to use it and protect it at the same time.

In this law, which is not subject to human repeal, is the justification of the small, family-owned, family-worked farm, for this law gives a preeminent and irrevocable value to *familiarity,* the family life that alone can properly connect a people to a land. This connection, admittedly, is easy to sentimentalize, and we must be careful not to do so. We all know that small family farms can be abused because we know that sometimes they have been; nevertheless, it is true that familiarity tends to mitigate and to correct abuse. A family that has farmed land through two or three generations will possess not just the land but a remembered history of its own mistakes and of the remedies of those mistakes. It will know, not just what it *can* do, what is technologically possible, but also what it *must* do and what it must *not* do;

the family will have understood the ways in which it and the farm empower and limit one another. This is the value of longevity in landholding: In the long term, knowledge and affection accumulate, and, in the long term, knowledge and affection pay. They do not just pay the family in goods and money; they also pay the family and the whole country in health and satisfaction.

But the justifications of the family farm are not merely agricultural; they are political and cultural as well. The question of the survival of the family farm and the farm family is one version of the question of who will own the country, which is, ultimately, the question of who will own the people. Shall the usable property of our country be democratically divided, or not? Shall the power of property be a democratic power, or not? If many people do not own the usable property, then they must submit to the few who do own it. They cannot eat or be sheltered or clothed except in submission. They will find themselves entirely dependent on money; they will find costs always higher, and money always harder to get. To renounce the principle of democratic property, which is the only basis of democratic liberty, in exchange for specious notions of efficiency or the economics of the so-called free market is a tragic folly.

There is one more justification, among many, that I want to talk about—namely, that the small farm of a good farmer, like the small shop of a good craftsman or craftswoman, gives work a quality and a dignity that it is dangerous, both to the worker and the nation, for human work to go without. If using ten workers to make one pin results in the production of many more pins than the ten workers could produce individually, that is undeniably an improvement in production, and perhaps uniformity is a virtue in pins. But, in the process, ten workers have been demeaned; they have been denied the economic use of their minds; their work has become thoughtless and skill-less. Robert Heilbroner says that such "division of labor reduces the activity of labor to dismembered gestures."[2]

As I noted above in "The Loss of the University," Eric Gill sees

in this industrial dismemberment of labor a crucial distinction
between *making* and *doing,* and he describes "the degradation of
the mind" that is the result of the shift from making to doing.[3]
This degradation of the mind cannot, of course, be without consequences. One obvious consequence is the degradation of products. When workers' minds are degraded by loss of responsibility
for what is being made, they cannot use judgment; they have no
use for their critical faculties; they have no occasions for the
exercise of workmanship, of workmanly pride. And the consumer is degraded by loss of the opportunity for qualitative
choice. This is why we must now buy our clothes and immediately resew the buttons; it is why our expensive purchases
quickly become junk.

With industrialization has come a general depreciation of
work. As the price of work has gone up, the value of it has gone
down, until it is now so depressed that people simply do not want
to do it anymore. We can say without exaggeration that the present national ambition of the United States is unemployment. People live for quitting time, for weekends, for vacations, and for
retirement; moreover, this ambition seems to be classless, as true
in the executive suites as on the assembly lines. One works, not
because the work is necessary, valuable, useful to a desirable end,
or because one loves to do it, but only to be able to quit—a
condition that a saner time would regard as infernal, a condemnation. This is explained, of course, by the dullness of the work,
by the loss of responsibility for, or credit for, or knowledge of the
thing made. What can be the status of the working small farmer
in a nation whose motto is a sigh of relief: "Thank God it's
Friday"?

But there is an even more important consequence: By the dismemberment of work, by the degradation of our minds as workers, we are denied our highest calling, for, as Gill says, "every man
is called to give love to the work of his hands. Every man is called
to be an artist."[4] The small family farm is one of the last places—
they are getting rarer every day—where men and women (and

girls and boys, too) can answer that call to be an artist, to learn to give love to the work of their hands. It is one of the last places where the maker—and some farmers still do talk about "making the crops"—is responsible, from start to finish, for the thing made. This certainly is a spiritual value, but it is not for that reason an impractical or uneconomic one. In fact, from the exercise of this responsibility, this giving of love to the work of the hands, the farmer, the farm, the consumer, and the nation all stand to gain in the most practical ways: They gain the means of life, the goodness of food, and the longevity and dependability of the sources of food, both natural and cultural. The proper answer to the spiritual calling becomes, in turn, the proper fulfillment of physical need.

The family farm, then, is good, and to show that it is good is easy. Those who have done most to destroy it have, I think, found no evil in it. But, if a good thing is failing among us, pretty much without being argued against and pretty much without professed enemies, then we must ask *why* it should fail. I have spent years trying to answer this question, and, while I am sure of some answers, I am also sure that the complete answer will be hard to come by because the complete answer has to do with who and what we are as a people; the fault lies in our identity and therefore will be hard for us to see.

However, we must *try* to see, and the best place to begin may be with the fact that the family farm is not the only good thing that is failing among us. The family farm is failing because it belongs to an order of values and a kind of life that are failing. We can only find it wonderful, when we put our minds to it, that many people now seem willing to mount an emergency effort to "save the family farm" who have not yet thought to save the family or the community, the neighborhood schools or the small local businesses, the domestic arts of household and homestead, or cultural and moral tradition—all of which are also failing, and on all of which the survival of the family farm depends.

The family farm is failing because the pattern it belongs to is failing, and the principal reason for this failure is the universal adoption, by our people and our leaders alike, of industrial values, which are based on three assumptions:

1. That value equals price—that the value of a farm, for example, is whatever it would bring on sale, because both a place and its price are "assets." There is no essential difference between farming and selling a farm.

2. That all relations are mechanical. That a farm, for example, can be used like a factory, because there is no essential difference between a farm and a factory.

3. That the sufficient and definitive human motive is competitiveness—that a community, for example, can be treated like a resource or a market, because there is no difference between a community and a resource or a market.

The industrial mind is a mind without compunction; it simply accepts that people, ultimately, will be treated as things and that things, ultimately, will be treated as garbage.

Such a mind is indifferent to the connections, which are necessarily both practical and cultural, between people and land; which is to say that it is indifferent to the fundamental economy and economics of human life. Our economy is increasingly abstract, increasingly a thing of paper, unable either to describe or to serve the real economy that determines whether or not people will eat and be clothed and sheltered. And it is this increasingly false or fantastical economy that is invoked as a standard of national health and happiness by our political leaders.

That this so-called economy can be used as a universal standard can only mean that it is itself without standards. Industrial economists cannot measure the economy by the health of nature, for they regard nature as simply a source of "raw materials." They cannot measure it by the health of people, for they regard people as "labor" (that is, as tools or machine parts) or as "consumers." They can measure the health of the economy only in sums of money.

Here we come to the heart of the matter—the absolute divorce that the industrial economy has achieved between itself and all ideals and standards outside itself. It does this, of course, by arrogating to itself the status of primary reality. Once that is established, all its ties to principles of morality, religion, or government necessarily fall slack.

But a culture disintegrates when its economy disconnects from its government, morality, and religion. If we are dismembered in our economic life, how can we be members in our communal and spiritual life? We assume that we can have an exploitive, ruthlessly competitive, profit-for-profit's-sake economy, and yet remain a decent and a democratic nation, as we still apparently wish to think ourselves. This simply means that our highest principles and standards have no practical force or influence and are reduced merely to talk.

That this is true was acknowledged by William Safire in a recent column, in which he declared that our economy is driven by greed and that greed, therefore, should no longer count as one of the seven deadly sins. "Greed," he said, "is finally being recognized as a virtue . . . the best engine of betterment known to man." It is, moreover, an agricultural virtue: "The cure for world hunger is the driving force of Greed." Such statements would be possible only to someone who sees the industrial economy as the ultimate reality. Mr. Safire attempts a disclaimer, perhaps to maintain his status as a conservative: "I hold no brief for Anger, Envy, Lust, Gluttony, Pride, Envy or Sloth."[5] But this is not a cat that can be let only partly out of the bag. In fact, all seven of the deadly sins are "driving forces" of this economy, as its advertisements and commercials plainly show.

As a nation, then, we are not very religious and not very democratic, and *that* is why we have been destroying the family farm for the last forty years—along with other small local economic enterprises of all kinds. We have been willing for millions of people to be condemned to failure and dispossession by the workings of an economy utterly indifferent to any claims they may have had either as children of God or as citizens of a democracy. "That's the way a dynamic economy works," we have said. We have said, "Get big or get out." We have said, "Adapt or die." And we have washed our hands of them.

Throughout this period of drastic attrition on the farm, we supposedly have been "subsidizing agriculture," but, as Wes Jackson has pointed out,[6] this is a misstatement. What we have actually been doing is using the farmers to launder money for the agribusiness corporations, which have controlled both their supplies and their markets, while the farmers have overproduced and been at the mercy of the markets. The result has been that the farmers have failed by the millions, and the agribusiness corporations have prospered—or they prospered until the present farm depression, when some of them have finally realized that, after all, they are dependent on their customers, the farmers.

Throughout this same desperate time, the colleges of agriculture, the experiment stations, and the extension services have been working under their old mandate to promote "a sound and prosperous agriculture and rural life," to "aid in maintaining an equitable balance between agriculture and other segments of the economy," to contribute "to the establishment and maintenance of a permanent and effective agricultural industry," and to help "the development and improvement of the rural home and rural life."[7]

That the land-grant system has failed this commission is, by now, obvious. I am aware that there are many individual professors, scientists, and extension workers whose lives have been dedicated to the fulfillment of this commission and whose work has genuinely served the rural home and rural life. But, in general, it can no longer be denied that the system as a whole has failed. One hundred and twenty-four years after the Morrill Act, ninety-nine years after the Hatch Act, seventy-two years after the Smith-Lever Act, the "industrial classes" are not liberally educated, agriculture and rural life are not sound or prosperous or permanent, and there is no equitable balance between agriculture and other segments of the economy. Anybody's statistics on the reduction of the farm population, on the decay of rural communities, on soil erosion, soil and water pollution, water shortages, and farm bankruptcies tell indisputably a story of failure.

This failure cannot be understood apart from the complex allegiances between the land-grant system and the aims, ambitions, and values of the agribusiness corporations. The willingness of land-grant professors, scientists, and extension experts to serve as state-paid researchers and traveling salesmen for those corporations has been well documented and is widely known.

The reasons for this state of affairs, again, are complex. I have already given some of them; I don't pretend to know them all. But I would like to mention one that I think is probably the most telling: that the offices of the land-grant complex, like the offices of the agricultural bureaucracy, have been looked upon by their aspirants and their occupants as a means, not to serve farmers, but to escape farming. Over and over again, one hears the specialists and experts of agriculture introduced as "old farm boys" who have gone on (as is invariably implied) to better things. The reason for this is plain enough: The life of a farmer has characteristically been a fairly hard one, and the life of a college professor or professional expert has characteristically been fairly easy. Farmers—working family farmers—do not have tenure, business hours, free weekends, paid vacations, sabbaticals, and retirement funds; they do not have professional status.

The direction of the career of agricultural professionals is, typically, not toward farming or toward association with farmers. It is "upward" through the hierarchy of a university, a bureau, or an agribusiness corporation. They do not, like Cincinnatus, leave the plow to serve their people and return to the plow. They leave the plow, simply, for the sake of leaving the plow.

This means that there has been for several decades a radical disconnection between the land-grant institutions and the farms, and this disconnection has left the land-grant professionals free to give bad advice; indeed, if they can get this advice published in the right place, from the standpoint of their careers it does not matter whether their advice is good or not.

For example, after years of milk glut, when dairy farmers are everywhere threatened by their surplus production, university experts are still working to increase milk production and still advising farmers to cull their least-productive cows—apparently oblivious both of the possible existence of other standards of judgment and of the fact that this culling of the least-productive cows is, ultimately, the culling of the smaller farmers.

Perhaps this could be dismissed as human frailty or inevitable bureaucratic blundering—except that the result is damage, caused by people who probably would not have given such advice if they were themselves in a position to suffer from it. Serious responsibilities are undertaken by public givers of advice, and serious wrong is done when the advice is bad. Surely a kind of monstrosity is involved when tenured professors with protected incomes recommend or even tolerate Darwinian economic policies for farmers, or announce (as one university economist after another has done) that the failure of so-called inefficient farmers is good for agriculture and good for the country. They see no inconsistency, apparently, between their own protectionist economy and the "free market" economy that they recommend to their supposed constituents, to whom the "free market" has proved, time and again, to be fatal. Nor do they see any inconsistency, apparently, between the economy of a university, whose sources, like those of any tax-supported institution, are highly diversified, and the extremely specialized economies that they have recommended to their farmer-constituents. These inconsistencies nevertheless exist, and they explain why, so far, there has been no epidemic of bankruptcies among professors of agricultural economics.

These, of course, are simply instances of the notorious discrepancy between theory and practice. But this discrepancy need not exist, or it need not be so extreme, in the colleges of agriculture. The answer to the problem is simply that those who profess should practice. Or at least a significant percentage of them should. This is, in fact, the rule in other colleges and departments of the university. A professor of medicine who was no doctor would readily be seen as an oddity; so would a law professor who could not try a case; so would a professor of architecture who could not design a building. What, then, would be so strange about an agriculture professor who would be, and who would be expected to be, a proven farmer?

But it would be wrong, I think, to imply that the farmers are merely the victims of their predicament and share none of the blame. In fact, they, along with all the rest of us, do share the blame, and their first hope of survival is in understanding that they do.

Farmers, as much as any other group, have subscribed to the industrial fantasies that I listed earlier: that value equals price, that all relations are mechanical, and that competitiveness is a proper and sufficient motive. Farmers, like the rest of us, have assumed, under the tutelage of people with things to sell, that selfishness and extravagance are merely normal. Like the rest of us, farmers have believed that they might safely live a life prescribed by the advertisers of products, rather than the life required by fundamental human necessities and responsibilities.

One could argue that the great breakthrough of industrial agriculture occurred when most farmers became convinced that it would be better to own a neighbor's farm than to have a neighbor, and when they became willing, necessarily at the same time, to borrow extravagant amounts of money. They thus violated the two fundamental laws of domestic or community economy: You must be thrifty and you must be generous; or, to put it in a more practical way, you must be (within reason) independent, and you must be neighborly. With that violation, farmers became vulnerable to everything that has intended their ruin.

An economic program that encourages the unlimited growth of individual holdings not only anticipates but actively proposes the failure of many people. Indeed, as our antimonopoly laws testify, it proposes the failure, ultimately, of all but one. It is a fact, I believe, that many people have now lost their farms and are out of farming who would still be in place had they been willing for their neighbors to survive along with themselves. In light of this, we see that the machines, chemicals, and credit that farmers have been persuaded to use as "labor savers" have, in fact, performed as neighbor replacers. And whereas neighborhood tends to work as a service free to its members, the machines, chemicals, and credit have come at a cost set by people who were *not* neighbors.

That is a description of the problem of the family farm, as I see it. It is a dangerous problem, but I do not think it is hopeless. On the contrary, a number of solutions to the problem are implied in my description of it.

What, then, can be done?

The most obvious, the most desirable, solution would be to secure that "equitable balance between agriculture and other segments of the economy" that is one of the stated goals of the Hatch Act. To avoid the intricacies of the idea of "parity," which we inevitably think of here, I will just say that the price of farm products, as they leave the farm, should be on a par with the price of those products that the farmer must buy.

In order to achieve this with minimal public expense, we must control agricultural production; supply must be adjusted to demand. Obviously this is something that individual farmers, or individual states, cannot do for themselves; it is a job that belongs appropriately to the federal government. As a governmental function, it is perfectly in keeping with the ideal, everywhere implicit in the originating documents of our government, that the small have a right to certain protections from the great. We have, within limits that are obvious and reasonable, the *right* to be small farmers or small businessmen or -women, just as, or perhaps insofar as, we have a right to life, liberty, and property. The individual citizen is not to be victimized by the rich any more than by the powerful. When Marty Strange writes, "To the extent that only the exceptional succeed, the system fails,"[8] he is economically, and agriculturally sound, but he is also speaking directly from American political tradition.

The plight of the family farm would be improved also by other governmental changes—for example, in policies having to do with taxation and credit.

Our political problem, of course, is that farmers are neither numerous enough nor rich enough to be optimistic about government help. The government tends, rather, to find their surplus production useful and their economic failure ideologically desirable. Thus, it seems to me that we must concentrate on those things that farmers and farming communities can do for themselves—striving in the meantime for policies that would be desirable.

It may be that the gravest danger to farmers is their inclination to look to the government for help, after the agribusiness corporations and the universities (to which they have already looked) have failed them. In the process, they have forgotten how to look to themselves, to their farms, to their families, to their neighbors, and to their tradition.

Marty Strange has written also of his belief "that commercial agriculture can survive within pluralistic American society, as we know it—*if* [my emphasis] the farm is rebuilt on some of the values with which it is popularly associated: conservation, independence, self-reliance, family, and community. To sustain itself, commercial agriculture will have to reorganize its social and economic structure as well as its technological base and production methods in a way that reinforces these values."[9] I agree. Those are the values that offer us survival, not just as farmers, but as human beings. And I would point out that the transformation that Marty is proposing cannot be accomplished by the governments, the corporations, or the universities; if it is to be done, the farmers themselves, their families, and their neighbors will have to do it.

What I am proposing, in short, is that farmers find their way out of the gyp joint known as the industrial economy.

The first item on the agenda, I suggest, is the remaking of the rural neighborhoods and communities. The decay or loss of these has demonstrated their value; we find, as we try to get along without them, that they are worth something to us—spiritually, socially, and economically. And we hear again the voices out of our cultural tradition telling us that to have community, people don't need a "community center" or "recreational facilities" or any of the rest of the paraphernalia of "community improvement" that is always for sale. Instead, they need to love each other, trust each other, and help each other. That is hard. All of us know that no community is going to do those things easily or perfectly, and yet we know that there is more hope in that difficulty and imperfection than in all the neat instructions for getting big and getting rich that have come out of the universities and the agribusiness corporations in the past fifty years.

Second, the farmers must look to their farms and consider the losses, human and economic, that may be implicit in the way those farms are structured and used. If they do that, many of them will understand how they have been cheated by the industrial orthodoxy of competition—how specialization has thrown them into competition with other farmer-specialists, how bigness of scale has thrown them into competition with neighbors and friends and family, how the consumer economy has thrown them into competition with themselves.

If it is a fact that for any given farm there is a ratio between people and acres that is correct, there are also correct ratios between dependence and independence and between consumption and production. For a farm family, a certain degree of independence is possible and is desirable, but no farmer and no family can be entirely independent. A certain degree of dependence is inescapable; whether or not it is desirable is a question of who is helped by it. If a family removes its dependence from its neighbors—if, indeed, farmers remove their dependence from their families—and give it to the agribusiness corporations (and to moneylenders), the chances are, as we have seen, that the farmers and their families will not be greatly helped. This suggests that dependence on family and neighbors may constitute a very desirable kind of independence.

It is clear, in the same way, that a farm and its family cannot be *only* productive; there must be some degree of consumption. This, also, is inescapable; whether or not it is desirable depends on the ratio. If the farm consumes too much in relation to what it produces, then the farm family is at the mercy of its suppliers and is exposed to dangers to which it need not be exposed. When, for instance, farmers farm on so large a scale that they cannot sell their labor without enormous consumption of equipment and supplies, then they are vulnerable. I talked to an Ohio farmer recently who cultivated his corn crop with a team of horses. He explained that, when he was plowing his corn, he was *selling* his labor and that of his team (labor fueled by the farm itself and, therefore, very cheap) rather than *buying* herbicides. His point was simply that there is a critical difference between buying and selling and that the name of this difference at the year's end ought to be net gain.

Similarly, when farmers let themselves be persuaded to buy their food instead of grow it, they become consumers instead of producers and lose a considerable income from their farms. This is simply to say that there is a domestic economy that is proper to the farming life and that it is different from the domestic economy of the industrial suburbs.

Finally, I want to say that I have not been talking from speculation but from proof. I have had in mind throughout this essay the one example known to me of an American community of small family farmers who have not only survived but thrived during some very difficult years: I mean the Amish. I do not recommend, of course, that all farmers should become Amish, nor do I want to suggest that the Amish are perfect people or that their way of life is perfect. What I want to recommend are some Amish principles:

1. They have preserved their families and communities.

2. They have maintained the practices of neighborhood.

3. They have maintained the domestic arts of kitchen and garden, household and homestead.

4. They have limited their use of technology so as not to displace or alienate available human labor or available free sources of power (the sun, wind, water, and so on).

5. They have limited their farms to a scale that is compatible both with the practice of neighborhood and with the optimum use of low-power technology.

6. By the practices and limits already mentioned, they have limited their costs.

7. They have educated their children to live at home and serve their communities.

8. They esteem farming as both a practical art and a spiritual discipline.

These principles define a world to be lived in by human beings, not a world to be exploited by managers, stockholders, and experts.

NOTES

1. In conversation.
2. Robert Heilbroner, "The Act of Work," Occasional Paper of the Council of Scholars (Washington, D.C.: Library of Congress, 1984), p. 20.
3. Eric Gill, *A Holy Tradition of Working* (Suffolk, England: Golgonooza Press, 1983), p. 61.
4. Ibid., p. 65.
5. William Safire, "Make That *Six* Deadly Sins—A Re-examination Shows Greed to Be a Virtue," Courier-Journal (Louisville, Ky.), 7 Jan., 1986.
6. In conversation.
7. Hatch Act, United States Code, Section 361b.
8. Marty Strange, "The Economic Structure of a Sustainable Agriculture," in *Meeting the Expectations of the Land,* ed. Wes Jackson, Wendell Berry, and Bruce Colman (San Francisco: North Point Press, 1984), p. 118.
9. Ibid., p. 116.

Does Community
Have a Value?

1986

Community is a concept, like humanity or peace, that virtually no one has taken the trouble to quarrel with; even its worst enemies praise it. There is almost no product or project that is not being advocated in the name of community improvement. We are told that we, as a community, are better off for the power industry, the defense industry, the communications industry, the transportation industry, the agriculture industry, the food industry, the health industry, the medical industry, the insurance industry, the sports industry, the beauty industry, the entertainment industry, the mining industry, the education industry, the law industry, the government industry, and the religion industry. You could look into any one of these industries and find many people, some of them in influential positions, who are certifiably "community spirited."

In fact, however, neither our economy, nor our government, nor our educational system runs on the assumption that community has a value—a value, that is, that *counts* in any practical or powerful way. The values that are assigned to community are emotional and spiritual—"cultural"—which makes it the subject of pieties that are merely vocal. But does community have a value that is practical or economic? Is community necessary? If it does not have a value that is practical and economic, if it is not necessary, then can it have a value that is emotional and spiritual? Can "community values" be preserved simply for their own sake? Can people be neighbors, for example, if they do not need each other or help each other? Can there be a harvest festival where there is no harvest? Does economy have spiritual value?

Such questions are being forced upon us now by the loss of community. We are discouraged from dealing with them by their difficulty in such a time as this, and yet these questions and others like them are indispensable to us, for they describe the work that we must do. We can only be encouraged to see that this work, though difficult, is fascinating and hopeful. It is homework, do-able in some part by everybody, useful to everybody—as far as possible unlike the massive, expensive, elitist projects that now engross virtually every government of the world.

But, before I go any farther, let me make clear what I mean by community. I will give as particular an example as I know.

My friends Loyce and Owen Flood married in October 1938, and moved to a farm in hilly country near Port Royal, Kentucky. She was seventeen; Owen was eighteen.

Loyce had graduated from high school and had been to college for a short while. Although she had been raised on a farm she did not know a great deal about being a farmer's wife on a small, poor, hillside place. She and Owen had little money, and she had to learn quickly the arts of subsistence.

Fortunately, they were living in a neighborhood of households closely bound together by family ties or friendships and by well-established patterns of work and pleasure. This neighborhood included, in varying degrees of intimacy and interdependence, nine households, all more or less within walking distance. The women kept house individually, but all the big jobs they did together: housecleaning, wallpapering, quilting, canning, cooking for field crews. Though Loyce looked up to these women and called them "Miss Suzy," "Miss Berthy," and so on, most of them were still fairly young, in their late thirties or early forties. They were a set of hearty, humorous, industrious women, who saw whatever was funny and loved to make up funny names for things.

They became Loyce's teachers, and now, nearly fifty years later, she remembers with warmth and pleasure their kindness to her and their care for her. They helped her to learn to cook and can, to work in the hog killing and in the field (for, at planting and harvest times, the women went to the field with the men); they looked after her when she was sick; they taught her practical things, and things having to do with their mutual womanhood and community life. Although she had more formal schooling than any of them, she says now, "Everything I know I learned from those people." And the men were as kind and useful to Owen as the women were to Loyce. "They took us under their wing," she says.

The men farmed their own farms, but, like the women, they did the big jobs together. And when they worked together, they ate together. They always had a big dinner. "They never shirked dinner," Loyce says, "that was one thing sure." In hot weather, chicken would be the only fresh meat available, and they ate a lot of chicken. The women were perfectionists at making noodles.

By our standards now, these people were poor. The farms ranged in size from thirty-seven to perhaps a hundred acres. But only the thirty-seven-acre farm was entirely tillable. The others included a lot of "hill and holler." Then, as now, most of the money made on the produce of that place was made by manufacturers and merchants in other places; probably no household grossed more than $1,000 a year. The subsistence economy was necessarily elaborate and strong. The people raised and slaughtered their own meat, raised vegetable gardens, produced their own milk, butter, and eggs. They gathered the wild fruit as it ripened. They canned and dried and cured and preserved. They spent little money. The cash for the household came mainly from the sale of cream, and each farm kept three or four milk cows for that purpose. Loyce remembers that her weekly cream check was three dollars; they budgeted half of that for groceries and gasoline for the car and half for payment on a debt.

These people worked hard, and without any modern conveniences or labor savers. They had no tractors, no electricity, no refrigerators, no washing machines, no vacuum cleaners. Their one luxury was the telephone party line, which cost fifty cents a month. But their work was in limited quantities; they did not work at night or away from home; they knew their work, they knew how to work, and they knew each other. Loyce says, "They didn't have to do a lot of explaining."

Their work was mingled with their amusement; sometimes it *was* their amusement. Talk was very important: They worked together and talked; they saw each other in Port Royal on Saturday night and talked; on Sunday morning they went to church early and stood around outside and talked; when church was over, they talked and were in no hurry to go home.

In the summer they would get fifty pounds of ice and make ice cream, and eat the whole freezer full, and sometimes make another, and eat that. In the winter they would all go to somebody's house at night and pop corn, and the men would play cards and the women would talk. They played cards a lot. One of the households had books that could be borrowed. Loyce's private amusements were reading and embroidery. She does not remember ever getting lonesome or bored.

There are, as I see it, two salient facts about this neighborhood of 1938:
1. It was effective and successful as a community. It did what we know that a good community does: It supported itself, amused itself, consoled itself, and passed its knowledge on to the young. It was something to build on.

2. It no longer exists. By the end of World War II, it was both reduced and altered, and the remnants of its old life are now mainly memories.

The reasons why it no longer exists are numerous and complexly interrelated. Some of them are: increased farm income during and after the war; improved roads and vehicles; the influence of radio and then of television; rising economic expectations; changing social fashions; school consolidation; and the rapid introduction of industrial technology into agriculture after the war. And so the disappearance of this community into the modern world and the industrial economy is both a fact and, to a considerable extent, an understandable fact.

But we must take care not to stop with the mere recognition and understanding of facts. We must go ahead to ask if the fact exists for our good, if it can be understood to our good, and if its existence is necessary or inescapable. After establishing that a community has died, for example, we must ask who has been served by its death.

Such a community as I have described has often been caricatured and ridiculed and often sentimentalized. But, looked at in its facts, as my friend recalls them, it escapes both extremes. The people were manifestly equal to their lot; they were not oafish or stupid. On the other hand, they were not perfect; they were not living an idyll. The community was not immune either to change or to the need to change. Anyone familiar with the history of farming on Kentucky hillsides knows its practices could always have been improved.

But another fact that we must now reckon with is that this community did not change by improving itself. It changed by turning away from itself, from its place, from its own possibility. Somehow the periphery exhausted and broke the center. This community, like thousands of similar ones, was not changed by anything that *it* thought of, nor by anything thought of by anybody who believed that community had a practical or an economic value. It was changed, partly to its own blame, by forces, originating outside itself, that did not consider, much less desire, the welfare or the existence of such communities. This community, like any other, had to change and needed to change, but what if its own life, its own good, had been the standard by which it changed, rather than the profit of distant entrepreneurs and corporations?

We are left with questions—that one and others.

Is such a community desirable? My answer, unhesitatingly, is yes. But that is an answer notoriously subject to the charge of sentimentality or nostalgia. People will ask if I "want to turn back the clock." And so I am pushed along to another question, a more interesting one: Is such a community necessary? Again, I think, the answer must be yes, and here we have access to some manner of proof.

For one thing, the place once occupied by that community is now occupied by people who are not, in the same close, effective sense, a community. The place is no longer central to its own interest and its own economy. The people do not support themselves so much from the place or so much by mutual work and help as their predecessors did; they furnish much less of their own amusement and consolation; purchasing has more and more replaced growing and making; and less and less of local knowledge and practical skill is passed on to the young. In 1938, the community and its economy were almost identical. Today, the community is defined mostly by the mere proximity of its people to one another. The people belong, often to their own detriment, to a *national* economy whose centers are far from home.

For another thing, we now have before us the failure of the industrial system of agriculture that supplanted the community and the ways of 1938. There is, so far as I am aware, no way of denying the failure of an agricultural system that destroys both land and people, as the industrial system is now doing. Obviously, we need a way of farming that attaches people to the land much more intimately, carefully, and democratically than the industrial system has been able to do, and we can neither establish good farming nor preserve it without successful communities.

It is easy to suppose, as many powerful people apparently have done, that the principle of subsistence on family farms and in rural communities will be bad for the larger economy, but this supposition has proved to be a dangerous and destructive error. Subsistence is bad for the industrial economy and for the paper economy of the financiers; it is good for the actual, real-world economy by which people live and are fed, clothed, and housed. For example, in 1938, in the time of subsistence, there were three thriving grocery stores that were patronized by the neighborhood I have been talking about—one at Drennon's Lick and two at Port Royal. Now there is only one, at Port Royal. The "standard of living" (determined, evidently, by how much money is spent) has increased, but community life has declined, economically and every other way. In the neighborhoods around Port Royal, we now have many modern conveniences, but we buy and pay for them farther and farther from home. And we have fewer and fewer people at home who know how to maintain these conveniences and keep them running. Port Royal, in other words, now exists for "the economy"—that abstract accumulation of monetary power that aggrandizes corporations and governments and that does not concern itself at all for the existence of Port Royal.

For many years, I think, the people of rural America have been struggling with the realization that we are living in a colony. It is an irony especially bitter for Americans that, having cast off the colonialism of England, we have proceeded to impose a domestic colonialism on our own land and people, and yet we cannot deny that most of the money made on the products that we produce in rural America—food and fiber, timber, mineable fuels and minerals of all kinds—is made by other people in other places. We cannot deny that all of these fundamental enterprises, as now conducted, involve the destruction of the land and the people. We cannot deny that there is no provision being made and no thought being taken in any segment of the rural economy for the long-term welfare of the people who are doing the work. Indeed, we cannot deny that our leaders appear to take for granted that the eventual destruction of lives, livelihoods, homes, and communities is an acceptable, though not a chargeable, cost of production. The washed-out farm and bankrupt farmer, the strip-mined mountain and the unemployed or diseased miner, the clear-cut forest and the depressed logging town—all are seen as the mere natural results of so-called free enterprise. The pattern of industrial "development" on the farm and in the forest, as in the coal fields, is that of combustion and exhaustion—not "growth," a biological metaphor that is invariably contradicted by industrial practice.

The fault of a colonial economy is that it is dishonest; it misrepresents reality. In practice, it is simply a way of keeping costs off the books of an exploitive interest. The exploitive interest is absent from the countryside exactly as if the countryside were a foreign colony. The result of this separation is that the true costs of production are not paid by the exploitive interest but only suffered by the exploited land and people. The colony, whether foreign or domestic, becomes unstable, both as an ecosystem and as a community because colonialism does not permit the development of strong local economies. The economy of a colony exports only "raw material" and imports only finished goods. It buys and sells on markets over which it has no control; thus, both markets drain value from the colony. The economy of a colony is thus as far as possible from E. F. Schumacher's just (and safe) ideal of "local production from local resources for local use."

The way that a national economy preys on its internal colonies is by the destruction of community—that is, by the destruction of the principle of local self-sufficiency not only in the local economy but also in the local culture. Thus, local life becomes the dependent—indeed, the victim—not just of the food industry, the transportation industry, the power industries, the various agribusiness industries, and so on, but also of the entertainment, the education, and the religion industries—all involving change from goods once cheap or free to expensive goods having to be bought.

That the economy of most of rural America is a colonial economy became plain as soon as the local economies of subsistence lapsed and were replaced by the so-called "consumer economy." The old local economies of subsistence, which in America were often incomplete and imperfect, were nevertheless sources of local strength and independence, and, as I have suggested, they were a beginning on which we could have built. Their replacement by the "consumer economy" has brought a helpless dependence on distant markets, on transported manufactured goods, on cash, and on credit.

Even so cursory a description of one of the old local subsistence economies as I gave at the beginning of this essay reveals that its economic assets were to a considerable extent intangible: culture-borne knowledge, attitudes, and skills; family and community coherence; family and community labor; and cultural or religious principles such as respect for gifts (natural or divine), humility, fidelity, charity, and neighborliness. Such economies, furthermore, were mainly sun-powered, using plants and the bodies of animals and humans as "solar converters." By means of neighborhood, knowledge, and skill, they were turning free supplies to economic advantage. Theirs was an economy that took place, largely, off the books. The wonderful fact, then, is that those emotional and spiritual values that are now so inconsequentially associated with the idea of community were economic assets in the old communities, and they produced economic results.

This finding can be corroborated by an example that is contemporary, though somewhat more removed from my own acquaintance and culture. David Kline and his family, who are members of one of the Amish communities in the hilly country of eastern Ohio, have a farm of 123 acres that, even in the present hard times, is successful, both economically and agriculturally. It is one of the farms that, in my thinking about agriculture, I have used as a standard.

Of the Klineses' 123 acres, seventy-five are arable, twenty-nine are in permanent pasture, ten are forested, five are in orchard and gardens, and four are occupied by buildings. The major money-making enterprises of the farm are a dairy of twenty-three Guernsey cows (with about an equal number of heifers), and seven brood sows and a boar. The field crops, raised mainly to be fed on the place, are hay, corn, oats, and wheat. There are also the orchard and gardens, fifty laying hens, fifty pullets, fifty roosters for the table, and seven hives of bees. The farm combines commercial and subsistence enterprises, and its subsistence or household economy is obviously strong, producing some marketable surplus. In addition to the family's subsistence, this farm has been grossing about $50,000 a year and netting $25,000 to $30,000. In 1985, the gross was $47,000, and the net $25,000. In the midst of an agricultural depression, this is a startling accomplishment. Again, it is an economic result that is only somewhat computable; it is accounted for, in part, by the religious, cultural, family, and community coherence that is still maintained by the Old Order Amish, whose way of life, including their technology, makes possible the maximum utilization of natural (and therefore cheap or free) energy and fertility. A *full* accounting of David and Elsie Kline's economy would have to consider, as well, the extensive substitutions of natural and cultural gifts for purchased supplies.

That David Kline is also an excellent conservationist and a naturalist, who may delay a hay-cutting in order to allow bobolink fledglings to leave the nest, makes him even more useful to us as an example. For a part of the Amish understanding of good work, built into their technology and their methods, is this respect for nature. Farming, to the Klines, is the proper husbanding of nature, a stewardly care for the natural integrities and processes that precede and support the life of the farm.

David once attended a conference on the subject of community. What is community, the conferees were asking, and how can we have it? At some point, late in the proceedings, they asked

David what community meant to him. He said that when he and his son were plowing in the spring he could look around him and see seventeen teams at work on the neighboring farms. He knew those teams and the men driving them, and he knew that if he were hurt or sick, those men and those teams would be at work on his farm.

Conditioned as we all are now by industrial assumptions, we must be careful not to miss or to underestimate the point of David's reply: It is a practical description of a spiritual condition. With the Amish, economy is not merely a function of community; the community and the economy are virtually the same. We might, indeed, call an Amish community a loving economy, for it is based on the love of neighbors, of creatures, and of places. The community accomplishes the productive work that is necessary to any economy; the economy supports and preserves the land and the people. The economy cannot prey on the community because it is not alienated from the community; it *is* the community. We should notice, too, that David has described the economic helpfulness, the charity, that is natural to the life of a community—and free to members—that has been replaced, among most of the rest of us, by the insurance industry.

But let us go a little further and speculate on the relation between a subsistence-based family economy, such as the Klineses', and a local—say, a county—economy. It is easy to assume, as I have said, that a subsistence-based family economy would be bad for the larger economy of the locality or county. But let us put beside the Kline farm an industrial Ohio farm of 640 acres (or one square mile), and let us say that this farm grosses $200,000 and nets $20,000. (I think that those are safe figures for our purpose, for midwestern industrial farmers have often found it impossible to net 10 percent of gross.) This square mile of land is one farm, farmed by one family, and therefore dependent on large-scale equipment. For years, as the people have been leaving the farms and the farms have been getting larger, the suppliers and servicers of farm machines, which have also been getting larger, have been withdrawing toward the larger towns. Now industrial farmers must sometimes drive astonishing distances for parts and repairs. For the farmer of a large industrial farm, the economic center has thus moved far beyond the local community, and we must suppose that a large percentage of his operating costs goes outside the local community.

But a square mile of even reasonably good land would contain five farms more or less the size of the Klineses'. If we suppose that the families would average three children each, this would increase the human population of the square mile from five to twenty-five. Such an increase in population implies a reduction in the scale of equipment, which in turn implies an increase of business for local suppliers and mechanics. Moreover, the population increase implies an increase of business for local shops and businesses of all kinds. If we use the Klines' farm economy as a base and suppose that the five farms average $50,000 a year gross and $25,000 a year net, then we see that they increase the gross income of the square mile by only $50,000. But, individually, the five farms each would net $5,000 a year more than the large farm, and together they would increase the net income on the square mile to $125,000, an increase of net over the large single farm of $105,000.

This comparison is not entirely speculative; Marty Strange says, for instance, that in Iowa, in the years 1976–1983, small farms achieved "*more* output per dollar invested" than large farms. "In fact," he says, "the larger the farm, the lower the output per dollar invested." However, since my comparison must be at least partly speculative, I can hope only to suggest a possibility that has been ignored: that strong communities imply strong local economies and vice versa—that, indeed, strong communities and strong local economies are identical.

Does this mean that, as local economies grow strong, there must be a concomitant weakening of the national economy? I do not think so. Strong local economies everywhere would, it seems to me, inevitably add up to strong national economies and to a strong world economy. The necessary distinction here is between temporary and permanent economic strength. A national economy may burgeon at the expense of its local economies, as ours has been doing, but, obviously, it can do so only for a while. The permanence of a national economy, we may be sure, would not be measurable by "gross national product," which may, after all, involve local net deficits of, say, topsoil or underground water. It would have to be measured by the health of its communities, both human and natural.

If these communities are given no standing in the computations, then all costs and benefits to and from the community are "externalized," and a business may show a profit to everybody else's loss. The cost of community to each of its members is restraint, limitation of scale. Its benefits, within acceptance of that limitation, are the many helps, human and natural, material and otherwise, that a community makes freely or cheaply available to its members. If an appropriate limitation of scale is not accepted, then the community is simply replaced by large-scale operators who work in isolation and by the dispossessed and excluded poor, who do not stay in place but drift into the cities where they are counted, no longer as "surplus" farmers (or miners or woods workers), but as "unemployed."

If the human and natural communities are given no standing in the computations, then the large farm or other large enterprise acts as a siphon to drain economic and other values out of the locality into the "gross national product." This happens because its technology functions on behalf of the national economy, not the local community.

The bait that has opened communities to exploitation and destruction has always been ready cash for local people. But there has never been as much cash forthcoming to the local people as to people elsewhere—not by far. The supply of ready cash has tended to be undependable or temporary, and it has usually come as a substitute for things more permanent and dearer than cash, and harder to replace, once lost.

The only preventive and the only remedy is for the people to choose one another and their place, over the rewards offered them by outside investors. The local community must understand itself finally as a community of interest—a common dependence on a common life and a common ground. And because a community is, by definition, *placed*, its success cannot be divided from the success of its place, its natural setting and surroundings: its soils, forests, grasslands, plants and animals, water, light, and air. The two economies, the natural and the human, support each other; each is the other's hope of a durable and a livable life.

Printed in the United States
44458LVS00001B/117

9 780865 472754